HYPNOTHERAPY ASSERTIONS AND AFFIRMATIONS FOR CHRISTIANS

OVERCOMING OUR MANY HEALTH ISSUES & EXPANDING OUR MINDS

Dr. Lauren J. Ball

WESTBOW
P R E S S®
A DIVISION OF THOMAS NELSON
& ZONDERVAN

WestBow Press books may be ordered through booksellers or by contacting:

WestBow Press
A Division of Thomas Nelson & Zondervan
1663 Liberty Drive
Bloomington, IN 47403
www.westbowpress.com
1 (866) 928-1240

ISBN: 978-1-9736-1538-5 (sc)
ISBN: 978-1-9736-1537-8 (e)

Print information available on the last page.

WestBow Press rev. date: 03/08/2018

Contents

Dedication

THIS BOOK IS DEDICATED TO those who are searching for a better, healthier life filled with happiness and a desire to serve our Lord and Savior, and humanity in a world, which has mostly forgotten what it is like to be forgiving, loving, kind compassionate and giving. This world seems to be leaving behind many of the qualities mentioned above, for a more worldly existence, ignoring the Christ-like qualities, that makes this world a more peaceful, serene, and safer place in which to live and raise our children as true followers of Christ.

If there was ever a time in history that needs more spirituality, and less egocentrism, I have not heard of it. It appears that the children of this generation are more interested in their communication devises than eye-to eye communication. I'm afraid this will lead to a terrible vacuum that will be filled with socially unacceptable actions.

It is my prayer that this book will make a difference in those lives who are following the precepts taught in the living Gospel. We as a nation, surely need more love for our fellow man in these trying times just prior to the Savior's second coming.

I do hope you enjoy reading and using these pages as much as I did in penning them.

Preface

FAITH IS A BLESSING, FROM God, that must be accepted and used in every facet of the processes depicted in this work. Without faith, little would be accomplished by actively participating in any of the methods listed below. Faith will help the reader, identify, overcome, conquer and rise above the impediments and afflictions of life, with the help of God and bring the participants of this work better health and vitality.

Faith has its own difficulties to overcome; doubt being the greatest opposition to any accomplishment. Feelings of being unworthy and undeserving are almost as undesirable. I invite the students to use the assertions, (takes two people one to read, one to listen) and affirmations, (one person only), listed below to help counter the effects of doubt, unworthiness and undeserving, before attempting any of the other therapy units listed later. This insures the participants of enjoying the maximum results by taking full advantage of the therapies listed in this composition.

Each assertion or affirmation selected should be repeated at least four or five times for each session. Two assertions or two affirmations comprise a session. Each session should be reiterated, mornings and evenings, for four weeks, to reinforce their effectiveness.

Prologue

Since I have been practicing the profession of Chiropractic I have been interested, not only in helping to relieve physical pain and suffering, but also devise methods to alleviate mental and emotional problems. After much trial and error I have developed the methods outlined in this book and used them to help ease my patients suffering. Using the precepts described herein, gives the reader an opportunity for a better, happier life filled with less mental, emotional suffering and discomfort.

Those who are familiar with affirmations, will be delighted to find it enlightening to experience a whole new approach by using God, Jesus Christ and the Holy Ghost to aid them in the process of eliminating many of their mental disorders and illnesses.

I have also introduced a new concept, (assertions), involving two people, one as the Reader or voice, and another, the receiver, who accepts the information to help him/her overcome phobias, addictions, destructive traits, and many other undesirable problems.

The chapter on hypnotherapy, is briefly discussed, but is more for the licensed professionals. It is my intent to broaden the readers understanding of hypnotherapy and hypnosis and how they can be used to overcome, conquer, and rise above many of the ailments and problems, acquired in this life, always with the help of our divine Deities.

SELECT ONE OR TWO AFFIRMATIONS OR ASSERTIONS THEN RECITE ALOUD, PREFERABLY TO YOURSELF FOUR TIMES FOR EACH AFFIRMATION OR ASSERTION SELECTED. AFTER ONE MONTH SELECT ANOTHER ONE OR TWO DIFFERENT AFFIRMATIONS OR ASSERTIONS FOR MAXIMUM EFFECT.

BEFORE YOU BEGIN ANY OF THESE AFFIRMATIONS OR ASSERTIONS PLEASE ASK FATHER IN HEAVEN TO HELP YOU IN APPLYING THEM. WHEN YOU RECEIVE CONFERMATION

PROCEED. THE FOLLOWONG IS A PRAYER I USE TO GET MY CONFERMATION. OF COURSE YOU MAY USE A PRAYER OF YOUR OWN CHOOSING.

(FATHER IN HEAVEN BLESS ME WITH YOU'RE APPROVAL TO HELP ME EXPAND MY ABILITIES AND TO KNOW THAT I AM WORTHY OF, AND THAT I DESERVE THY HELP AS PRESENTED IN THESE AFFIRMATIONS AND ASSERTIONS? I ASK FOR THESE BLESSINGS IN THE NAME OF THY HOLY AND SACRED SON JESUS CHRST, AMEN.)

FATHER'S APLPROVAL MAY COME AS A GOOD GENTLE FEELING THAT THESE AFFIRMATIONS WILL HELP YOU TO IMPROVE YOUR STATE OF MIND PHICALLY, MENTALLY, EMOTIONALLY AND SPIRITUALLY.

THIS FIRST AFFIRMATION WILL HELP YOU TO PREPARE FOR THE MANY AFFIRMATIONS AND ASSERTIONS THAT FOLLOWS.

PLEASE USE THE DIFRECTIONS BEFORE EACH BLOC OF AFFIRMATIONS AND ASSERTIONS.

WITH THE INFINITELY POWERFUL HELP OF GOD, JESUS CHRIST, THE HOLY GHOST, AND WITH UNWAVERING FAITH, HUMILITY AND UNCONDITIONAL LOVE FOR THEM AND THEY FOR ME, I NOW THANK THEM FOR THEIR APPROVAL, WHICH THEY HAVE PREVIOUSLY GIVEN. I NOW PRAY THAT THEY WILL HELP ME BECOME HEALTHY AND HALE BY BLESSING ME WITH THE WILLINGNESS AND EAGERNESS TO RELEASE AND RELINQUISH ALL OF MY MENTAL, EMOTIONAL AND PHYSICAL HOLDS ON THE CAUSES AND ORIGINS OF MY ILLNESSES, MALADIES, AFFLICTIONS AND IMPERFECTIONS, SO I WILL BE RID OF THEM FOREVER, I NOW THANK HEAVENLY FATHER FOR ALL HIS HELP AND I AM NOW DEFINITELY DETERMINED TO HONOR THIS AFFIRMATION, WHICH WILL PENETRATE TO THE VERY DEPTHS OF MY SOUL AND SPIRIT. SO BE IT.

Chapter One

INTRODUCTION, HOW TO USE THIS MATERIAL

THIS BOOK WAS DESIGNED AS a self help book to not only bring us closer to Deity, but also help us overcome many of the maladies and ailments that plague each of us every day. To get the most good from the material herein, one should read this book from cover to cover, then select two of the assertions, or affirmations most needed, in your opinion, for help in identifying, overcoming, conquering, and rising above their negative effects on our minds and bodies. The selection should be beneficial to our spiritual growth and recited four or five times, with emphasis and conviction, morning and evening for a period of thirty days, and then select another unit for the next month, for the greatest effect.

Each affirmation should be uttered aloud to be most effective, however this is not always possible for some individuals in busy households, so an alternative of silently reciting them, to ourselves, with *feeling and meaning*, to be most effective.

The assertions should include someone, such as a spouse, or close friend that can be trusted, to recite the assertions you select.

Explicitly follow the directions given hereafter. The following four affirmations and assertions should be used next to acquaint the reader with the procedures necessary to get the maximum effect desired. Each affirmation should be uttered at least four times each morning and evening to be most effective, and for at least one month per unit.

AFFIRMATION # 1

I am now calling on the infinite power and eternal help of God, Jesus Christ, the Holy Ghost, and with absolute faith, gratitude, and unconditional love for them and they for me, and with my sincere prayers, and their approval, I believe I deserve to use my unwavering desire to overcome, conquer, and rise above the difficulties, and afflictions that prevents me from using my faith to perfect my righteous endeavors. I will now definitely forgive myself for not deserving this blessing. This is my commitment from this moment on and forever. I am determined to honor this affirmation, which will penetrate to the very depths of my soul and spirit. So be it.

AFFIRMATION # 2

I am now calling on the infinite power and eternal help of God, Jesus Christ, the Holy Ghost, and with absolute faith, gratitude, and unconditional love for them and they for me, and with my sincere prayers, and their approval, I now believe that I am of great worth and will use my new found faith to overcome, conquer, and rise above my adversities. This is my commitment from this moment on and forever. I am determined to honor this affirmation, which will penetrate to the very depths of my soul and spirit. So be it.

AFFIRMATION # 3

I am now calling on the infinite power and eternal help of God, Jesus Christ, the Holy Ghost, and with absolute faith, gratitude, and unconditional love for them and they for me, and with my sincere prayers, and with their approval, I have now conquered all my doubts and my faith is so strong that I can accomplish any righteous endeavor I set my set my mind to do. I will now definitely forgive myself of doubting my ability to use my faith to expunge all feelings of doubt, which allows me to overcome my afflictions. This is my commitment from this moment on and forever. I am determined to honor this affirmation, which will penetrate to the very depths of my soul and spirit. So be it.

AFFIRMATION # 4

I am now calling on the infinite power and eternal help of God, Jesus Christ, the Holy Ghost, and with absolute faith, gratitude, and unconditional love for them and they for me, and with my heartfelt, sincere prayers and their approval they will now help me to embrace and perfect the powerful element of faith. With conclusive determination, and irreversible willpower I will now positively act on this crucial decision from this moment on and forever. I am determined to honor this affirmation, which will penetrate to the very depths of my soul and spirit. So be it.

ASSERTION # 1

We are now calling on the infinite power and eternal help of God, Jesus Christ, the Holy Ghost, and with absolute faith, gratitude, and unconditional love for them and they for you and with your sincere prayers, and their approval, you know that you deserve to use your unwavering faith to overcome, conquer, and rise above the obstructions for using your faith to become whole again. You will now definitely forgive yourself of not deserving this blessing. This is your commitment from this moment on and forever. You are now determined to honor this, assertion, which, will penetrate to the very depths of your soul and spirit. So be it.

ASSERTION # 2

We are now calling on the infinite power and eternal help of God, Jesus Christ, the Holy Ghost, and with unwavering faith, gratitude, humility, and unconditional love for them and they for you, and with your sincere prayers, and their approval you now know that you are of great worth and that you will use your faith to, identify, overcome, conquer, and rise above the obstructions that prevent you from fully utilizing your faith to become whole again. You will now definitely forgive yourself of feeling unworthy and accept the blessing of faith to set you free of this encumbrance. This is your commitment from this moment on and forever. You are now determined to honor this assertion, which will penetrate to the very depths of your soul and spirit. So be it.

ASSERTION # 3

We are now calling on the infinite power and eternal help of God, Jesus Christ, the Holy Ghost, and with unwavering faith, gratitude, humility, and unconditional love for them and they for you and with your sincere prayers, and with their approval. You will now conquer all your doubts, and your faith is so strong that you can accomplish anything you set your mind to do. You will now definitely forgive yourself of doubting your ability to use your faith to expunge all feelings of doubt, which allows you to overcome your afflictions. This is your commitment from this moment on and forever. You will now thank heavenly father for all his help and are now definitely determined to honor this assertion, which will penetrate to the very depths of your soul and spirit. So be it.

ASSERTION # 4

We are now calling on the infinite power and eternal help of God, Jesus Christ, the Holy Ghost, and with unwavering faith, gratitude, humility, and unconditional love for them and they for you, and with your sincere, heartfelt prayers, and their approval they will now help you embrace and perfect the powerful element of faith. With absolute determination and irreversible willpower you will now positively act on this crucial decision from this moment on and forever. You will now definitely honor this assertion, which will penetrate to the very depths of your soul and spirit. So be it.

ON HYPNOSIS AND HYPNOTHERAPY

There is much mystery and mysticism surrounding hypnosis resulting in it being maligned, and misrepresented, by the media, which has misled the public and those who should be interested in using it for therapeutic purposes. The movie industry hasn't helped by portraying it as something evil, something to be avoided or shunned. Unfortunately the public, as a whole, has bought into this rhetoric and many have refused to accept it for what it is, a great tool to help with a myriad of physical, emotional, psychological, and even spiritual problems.

There is really nothing to fear from its righteous use, by those who are trained and qualified in its use to help individuals with their many problems. I hope this work will take away some of the mystery, mystique, and refute the misleading concepts presented by the media, and present the reader with an understanding of the true nature of hypnotherapy and the many benefits it offers. It is related to affirmations and assertions, and informs the readers how these may be used to live a more informed, pain and ailment free existence. Also, it can help one understand the source of many of our illnesses and dysfunctions, and how they may be expunged.

I have spent many years researching, condensing, selecting and rewriting this material, which would best serve those interested in these tools to advance the skills of healing and simplify the art and science of hypnotherapy, assertive-therapy and affirmation-therapy, each of which will occupy separate chapters. In assertive therapy, neither the voice, nor the receiver needs to be a professional therapist, since no trance is involved. Also, no in depth emotional therapy is involved. Chapter five helps the reader learn, through assertive-therapy, how to expunge many of the unrighteous elements of hate and destruction.

In chapter six we discuss assertive-therapy, to perfect many of the righteous elements of unity and love. We also discuss affirmations, which are strictly a one-person operation. Each unit is designed to help the reader perfect the elements of righteousness or eradicate the effects of the more trying problems, and emotional encumbrances. The reader selects, and preferably, reads aloud one or two units per session, four or five times with emotion, determination, and resolve, for the greatest effect.

I, personally, have used the methods outlined in these pages, on and off, for over sixty years, and have experienced a credible amount of success in their application. I do not advocate the use of hypnosis for theatrical entertainment because of the psychological and emotional harm that may, and has resulted, from its misuse.

THE INDUCTION AND THE METHOD of therapy selected, is the choice of the professional therapists, (psychologists and psychoanalysts), depending on the needs of the client or patient.

Recognizing and acknowledging that we create many of our diseases, illnesses and dysfunctions on a conscious and sub-conscious level, is of primary importance. It not only establishes us as the creators, but enables us to be, through these therapies, the dis-creators as well.

It is necessary, before we begin with the actual therapy, to understand some of the language and terms used by hypnotists and hypnotherapists:

Trance - A state resembling various stages of sleep, a condition or state of mind used in hypnosis to help a person accept certain suggestions which may help to alleviate pain, various ailments, mind and body dysfunctions, habits, addictions, phobias, memory problems, and many other ailments and afflictions, some of which are mentioned in detail later.

Induction - The process of placing a patient or client in a state of hypnotic sleep through, which they may become very susceptible to the mental acceptance of the hypnotist's healing suggestions.

Under - when the patient or client is in, or under one of the stages of hypnotic trance or sleep.

Hypnotic aids - devises that help the hypnotist put a client or patient into a trance. i.e. – the spiral wheel, candle, a pendulum, pulsating light, a moving object, soft music, or any other device or object that helps put the patient or client into one of the stages of trance, in which he or she becomes susceptible to suggestions.

Hypnotherapy - The art and science of helping a patient or client resolve problems, ailments, dysfunctions, illnesses, or afflictions through hypnosis. (Should be performed by a professional schooled in the use of hypnotherapy.)

Stages of trance – consecutively deeper states of hypnotic sleep, from light trance to a deep somnambulistic state. Ordinarily the light trance is sufficient for most subjects. For some a deeper state may be required.

Self Hypnosis – affirmations are an excellent form of self-hypnosis.

Assertive therapy – Therapy involving two persons: (the voice and the receiver) to reduce or eliminate minor psychological problems.

Regression –helping a patient or client regress back in time to where traumatic events have occurred that affects their health and wellbeing in an adverse way.

Units – The grouping of suggestions, assertions and affirmations, usually one paragraph; helps the client/patient resolve identified problem.

Chapter Two

·····◆·········▼·········◆·····

PRE-INDUCTION INFORMATION

BEFORE WE CAN IMPROVE OUR health, through these therapies, it is necessary to understand who we are.

Only by acknowledging and taking responsibility for our illnesses and ailments can we take the steps necessary to regain our health and help others do the same.

We are Quadra-energy entities comprised of physical, mental, emotional, and spiritual energies. These energies are responsible for the creation and maintenance of our health wellbeing, happiness and all other aspects of life. Our emotions control the levels and intensities of these energies.

Our bodies, minds, and spirits operate at different bio-electronic frequencies, pulsations, or vibrations, but in health, all possess an integrated, harmonic relationship. Our bodies, minds, and spirits operate at progressively higher energy levels, phases and frequencies and in health all work in a very close harmonic relationship.

These energies are comprised of harmonic frequencies or pulsations unique to each individual. Each person has a completely different operational, or functional frequency, pulsation and phase, than any other person in the world, but all life forms operate within the confines of very specific frequency ranges. Also within the basic life frequency each group of cells within each organ, tissue, and system that comprise our bodies, functions at different but harmonic frequencies. When illness and disease are present the frequencies or pulsations differ from healthy tissue, and harmony or wellness may no longer exist.

When the frequency, of any cells, tissues, organs, or systems in the body, is sufficiently altered by any, significant or sufficient, traumatic force, energy, or entity, illness and dysfunction will occur. Also as we age these frequencies diminish in amplitude or intensity, which usually results in various forms of illness and dysfunction.

Memories are comprised of stored, mental energies, images and frequencies consistent with their origin, intensity, and filtered by our five senses. Some are pro-life and others anti-life. The anti-life memories are caused by physical, emotional, or mental trauma in various forms and intensities. These anti-life frequencies interfere with the normal frequencies and are destructive to our health. The more intense the trauma the more likely we are to have serious illness and dysfunction in our cells, tissues, organs, and systems.

Many of our illnesses are caused by the failure of our internal response systems such as the immune system, digestive system, nervous system, etc. If these systems worked perfectly most of our illnesses would never occur. Many of our maladies are caused by improper diet, atmospheric and chemical toxins we inhale and ingest. It is a very complex problem but solvable by careful evaluation of our diets, exercise, sleep, and by reprograming our minds with the therapies and affirmations discussed herein.

The therapies and affirmations, discussed in this work consist of the repetitive reprograming of that portion of the brain that is responsible for our health and wellbeing. Essentially we repetitively suggest that our brains function in such a way that our health and vitality are returned or restored. This alone is not enough; we must also study and adhere to the essentials of diet, exercise, and emotional, spiritual, and mental health. Every element of health must be balanced and in harmony with the overall functions of our bodies, minds, and spirits. Treating only one of the elements of health will help, but still does not address the entire health problem. Just doing the Affirmations alone could help, but may not be enough. We must treat each and every element of health, to achieve the desired freedom from pain and illness.

To reiterate, it is imperative that we recognize and acknowledge, that we are the sole creators of many of our diseases, illnesses, and dysfunctions on a conscious and subconscious level. It not only establishes us as their creators, but also enables us to be free of the destructive effects of our unwanted and unneeded damaging creations by using the tools outlined here-in.

Through authoritative, authentic hypnotherapy, assertive-therapy, and affirmation-therapy, on a continuing daily basis, we will slowly, but surely impart to ourselves, clients, and therapists the desired results of better health and vitality. Just a single application or use of only one session of therapy or affirmation, will not help the client, patient or subject. Continued use every day, especially of the selected assertions and affirmations, will help to bring all of the client's physiological functions, in harmony and health. Vitality and happiness will surely follow.

Chapter Three

POST-INDUCTIVE INFORMATION

THE TRAUMA GENERATED BY ADVERSE, traumatic, physical and emotional experiences can produce fear, anxiety, anguish, guilt, anger, rage, shame, grudges, resentment, hatred, and non-forgiveness. If the events are intense enough, they may produce mental or emotional illness, or even physical illness. They may originate from accidents, or from physical punishment, undesirable behavior, like put-downs; i.e. (you will never amount to anything, why can't you do anything right, you are the most unattractive child I've ever seen, you are a bad girl/boy etc.) These usually come from of some authoritative source, such as mothers, fathers, siblings, aunts, uncles, spouses or other acquaintances or authoritative figures. Many of these traumas are so deeply rooted that hypnotherapy or other psychotherapies may be needed.

There are many different methods of placing a client/patient in a state of hypnotic trance. The therapist should be advised that there are several conditions to consider: Never break trust with your client/patient. Always explain what you are going to do and what this session will accomplish. Never touch a client without getting their permission. Never touch them inappropriately. Never do or say anything that would break trust. Breaking trust will deny the client/patient the opportunity of overcoming the purpose for the induction. Without trust the client/patient may not cooperate. Also, it could cause a distrust of all hypnotists and hypnotherapists. This distrust may cause the client/patient to fake a condition resembling a trance, and the goal of attaining help for him or her will not be achieved.

There is almost no end to the conditions and problems that hypnotherapy can relieve or benefit. A few of them are: addictions of all kinds, headaches, anesthesia, psychiatric problems, weight problems, memory problems, glandular imbalances, phobias of all kinds, many psychosomatic problems, and much, much more. The key to helping clients/patients overcome their problems is acquiring the knowledge of the many afflictions that beset mankind. Without the proper psychological, or psychiatric knowledge of these afflictions one could do the client/patient considerable long-term harm, which may be difficult to reverse. My advice is to let the trained professionals do their job.

Since my advice is to let the experts, function in their professions, I will not discuss the induction process since every specialist has his/her own favorite methods. My thrust will be to discuss some of the methods I have used, after the induction, with a substantial amount of success.

I always avoid all sexual overtones, or implied sexual phrases. I also avoid all traumatically oriented phrases or emotionally charged situations. Have client/patient avoid heavy meals or liquids for at least an hour before a session.

A visit to the restroom prior to the session may be needed. Nature's call will over-ride the induction.

Before the induction, I always ask the client; "are you willing to undergo hypnotherapy and accept all of my realistic suggestions to help rid yourself of the negative feelings and emotions associated with your parents and other sources that have impacted your life in a negative way?"

The therapist should never mentally traumatize their clients/patients. It may be advantageous, in the regression process, to place the client/patient in a state of isolation from trauma or emotional pain. One method I use is to place them in an imaginary, transparent bubble with four adjustable windows. While inside the bubble with the windows closed, inform them that no emotional pain can penetrate the bubble. This allows the client to view traumatic events from an emotionally pain free vantage point. Then, as therapy progresses, gradually, have them open one window at a time, allowing them to decrease the traumatic pain gradually, through suggestions, until, with all windows open, no emotional pain is felt. When the client/patient can view the events without emotional pain he or she is well on the way to diffusing the effects of the specific traumatic event. More than one session per source, or trauma may be needed to alleviate the problem. To accomplish this I go through a forgiveness process involving the source: mothers, fathers. Siblings, etc. and last of all forgiving self for what ever they feel they contributed to the traumatic event. Also have them forgive God for allowing this event to occur.

The major areas discussed here are some of the events, in childhood, that has created, psychological disabilities. These may include, but are not limited to the destructive actions of physical or mental abuse, molestation, violence, lying, or rape, etc. These actions will produce trauma, i.e. fear, guilt, anger, shame, grudges, resentment, hate, and non-forgiveness to name a few. The source is usually mothers, fathers, siblings, aunts, uncles, cousins, spouses, strangers and authority figures. Subconscious memories of these traumatic experiences, or events, are reinforced by repetitive recall, or the happening of similar events, and may cause many automatic, subconscious emotional responses and ailments.

The thrust of this section is to establish a pathway, through regression to each individual source, and trauma listed above. Through the process of self-forgiveness, and repetition, the therapist can expunge, diminish, reduce, or eliminate the effects of each event involving the sources and traumas listed above.

Because of the possible intensity of each traumatic event, more than one session per source, per event, may be needed to reduce, alleviate or expunge the trauma. It has been my experience that the client/patient should be in a state where no traumatic emotional pain exists, (with client in a bubble or similar vehicle), and should be gradually diminished during each session until no emotional pain exists. Each patient/client should be in a detached mode to view each event, which has caused the suffering. The therapist should use every one of the sources mentioned above, one at a time, to negate the effects of the trauma. Careful records and notes should always be kept to remind the therapist what has been done and what needs to be done.

You will observe that I have used various formats in both the assertions and the affirmations. There is, in my assessment, no single assertion or affirmation, which is better than any other. I have chosen these various formats to give the therapists and users what has worked for me. These are very powerful assertions and affirmations, but the readers may develop what works best for them. I have always included the deities, God, Jesus Christ and the Holy Ghost, in each assertion and affirmation so as to involve them in the great healing process, since they are the very source of all healing.

The following assertions should be used after the induction, and uttered with absolute conviction. Each assertion should be repeated four or five times with enthusiasm and persuasion. No more than two assertions or affirmations should ever be used in a single session.

Chapter Four

ASSERTIVE THERAPY UNITS

AFTER THE REGRESSION, THE FOLLOWING formats have been successfully used to help direct the, client/patient toward health and wellbeing:

> With the infinite power and eternal help of God, Jesus Christ, and the Holy Ghost, let my patient (give name) feel the sure knowledge that he/she is forgiven of his/her sins, indiscretions, and imperfections, which makes them worthy of thy blessings, especially thy great healing blessings. Let thy blessings of forgiveness wash over them and penetrate to their very souls. Also let thy blessings of worthiness, wash over them and allow them to know that they deserve thy love and blessings. Let all their doubts vanish. When their worthiness is assured, let their faith be magnified to the extent that they can forgive themselves and everyone of their trespasses against them. Let their judgment of others always be righteous. Let them be completely non-judgmental of everyone. Let their worthiness allow them to know that they deserve to be healed and that they will also have the power to heal those who come to them for help. You will now completely act on this decision from now on and forever.

You have now been regressed to the age when, with your source (mother), you had your first traumatic emotional experience. You will view this event from the safety of your transparent bubble, with all windows closed, where you will feel no emotional pain. With this sincere, heartfelt prayer you will overcome the emotional pain associated with this event:

> With the infinite power and eternal help of God, Jesus Christ, the Holy Ghost you will now forgive (name) for what he/she has caused, to create this event? You will now help him/her forgive his/her mother for the pain and trauma she has brought into his/her life with this event? In the sacred name of Jesus Christ, amen. Each time this suggestion is repeated and another window is opened you will feel less emotional pain. You will definitely act on this prompting from this moment on and forever.

(For the hypnotherapist. Each time you repeat this suggestion, have the client/patient open a window of the bubble to let diminished emotional pain be felt. Use this suggestion four or five times, before you conclude the session.

This same procedure should be applied for not only each source, but also for each traumatic event.

The next induction session for this patient should be with the father, and the next with each sibling, etc., until all of the childhood traumatic events have been addressed for each source.

The original procedure should be for early childhood up through adulthood.

Ensure that after each session the client/patient feels no more emotional pain. Any illness, or dysfunction, attributed to or associated with the traumatic event should then be eliminated.

Chapter Five

ASSERTIVE THERAPY UNITS (ELEMENTS OF HATE)

THE FOLLOWING ARE SOME OF the Christian oriented assertions, which should be very effective. Using the same format you may individualize the assertions to suit the needs of each individual. The thrust of this section is to use the voice of the reader to read each selected assertion to the receiver (the person being read to), so the assertions will be more viable.

ASSERTION #1

We are now calling on the infinite, powerful help of God, Jesus Christ, The Holy Ghost, and with unwavering faith, gratitude, humility, and unconditional love for them and they for you, and with their great healing power, and your, sincere, heartfelt prayers, and their approval, they will help you overcome the addiction of using tobacco: With the help of Deity, and upon your prayerful request, you will now forgive yourself for using tobacco and rid yourself of its destructive use and influence, which has adversely affected your life and health. You will never again feel the desire to use tobacco in any of its undesirable forms. You will feel that this addiction is so disgustingly repugnant, that the very thought of using tobacco will cause you to become ill. You will now definitely forgive yourself and all others who have helped you create and continue this offensive addiction. Your desires for its use, no longer exists. You will now completely rid yourself of this addiction from this moment on and forever. This assertion will now definitely penetrate to the very depths of your soul and spirit. So be it. (Repeat four or five times.)

ASSERTION # 2

We are now calling on the infinite power, and eternal help of God, Jesus Christ, the Holy Ghost, and with unwavering faith, gratitude, humility, and unconditional love for them and they for you, and with their great healing power, and your sincere, heartfelt prayers, and their approval, help you overcome this problem with food addiction: You will now forgive yourself of having a love for food, which causes this terrible addiction. You will now strive to understand why this condition persists and what you can do to eradicate it so you can enjoy a normal life. You will now eat a balanced diet; consisting of vegetables, fruits, protein, and lipids. Your Father in heaven will help you to overcome this terrible addiction if you sincerely ask Him. You will now completely rid yourself of this devastating afflictive addiction from now on and forever. You are now definitely determined to honor this assertion, which will penetrate to the very depths of your soul and spirit. So be it.

ASSERTION# 3

We are now calling on the infinite, eternal power and help of God, Jesus Christ, the Holy Ghost, and with unwavering faith, gratitude, humility and unconditional love for them and they for you, and with their great healing power, and your sincere, heartfelt prayers, and their approval, help you overcome these infirmities that has beset your brain with debilitating headaches, your eyes, your knee joint pain and degenerative problems. You will you now, absolutely, forgive yourself of what ever you believe you have done to create these illnesses. Father, please help him/her especially to be rid of the headache pain and your the knee pain. You will now completely act on this assertion, from this moment on and forever and will now definitely honor this assertion, which will penetrate to the very depth of your soul and spirit. So be it.

ASSERTION # 4

We are now calling on the infinite, eternal power and help of God, Jesus Christ, the Holy Ghost, and with unwavering faith, gratitude, humility, and unconditional love for them and they for you, and with their great healing power, and your sincere, heartfelt prayers, and their approval, They will help you overcome the addiction of using alcohol in any of its degenerative forms. You will now forgive yourself for using it and rid yourself of its destructive influence in any of its undesirable forms. You will feel that this addiction is so disgustingly repugnant, that the very thought of using it will cause you to become ill. You will now definitely forgive yourself and all others who have helped you create and continue this offensive addiction. Your desire for its use no longer exists. You now thank heavenly Father for all His help and you are now definitely determined to honor this assertion, which will penetrate to the very depths of your soul and spirit. So be it.

ASSERTION # 5

We are now calling on the infinite, eternal power and help of God, Jesus Christ, the Holy Ghost, and with unwavering faith, gratitude humility, and unconditional love for them and they for you, and with their great healing power, your sincere, heartfelt prayers, and their approval, they will help you overcome this drug addiction. You will now forgive yourself of using illegal drugs in any of their destructive, addictive forms. You will feel that this addiction is so disgustingly repugnant, that the very thought of using it will cause you to become ill. You will now definitely forgive yourself and all others who have helped you create and continue this offensive addiction. This decision is final from this moment on and forever. You now thank heavenly Father for all His help and you will definitely honor this assertion, which will penetrate to the very depths of your soul and spirit. So be it.

ASSERTION # 6

We are now calling on the infinite, eternal power and help of God, Jesus Christ, the Holy Ghost, and with unwavering faith, gratitude, humility, and unconditional love for them and they for you, and with their great healing power, and your sincere, heartfelt prayers, and their approval they will now help you rid yourself of the destructive influence of pornography and sex addiction. In fact, the very thought of involving yourself in these terribly offensive addictions will be so repugnant to you that you will become ill. You will now definitely forgive yourself and all others who have helped you create and continue this very unpleasant addiction. Your desire for its usage, thrills, and excitement, will decrease and diminish with each passing day until after one week, they will be so repulsive you will never again desire to engage in its use and will now completely embrace this noble assertion from this moment on and forever. Your decision is final. This assertion will penetrate to he very depths of your soul and spirit. So be it.

ASSERTION # 7

We are now calling on the infinite, eternal power and help of God, Jesus Christ, the Holy Ghost and with absolute faith, gratitude and unconditional love for them and they for you, and with their great healing power, your sincere, heartfelt prayers, and their approval they will now help you release the forces within you that prevent the great healing powers of God overcome your ailments. You will continually develop and use Gods great healing power in righteousness. Your desires for this great blessing will grow in magnitude each day until it is perfected. Always give the glory to God and Christ. You will now definitely honor this assertion, which will penetrate to the very depths of your soul and spirit. So be it.

ASSERTION # 8

We are now calling on the infinite, eternal, powerful forces of God, Jesus Christ, the Holy Ghost, and with, unwavering faith, gratitude, humility and unconditional love for them and they for you, with their great healing power, and your sincere, heartfelt prayers, and their approval, they will now help you release the destructive element, procrastination, within you, that holds you captive and prevents you from achieving your goals. Each day you will conquer this destructive power, and embrace all righteous powers that will set you free, and help you defeat the terrible urge to procrastinate. Your desires for this great blessing will increase each day until it no longer keeps you from righteous achievements. You will completely accept this noble assertion from this moment on and forever. You are now determined to honor this assertion, which will penetrate to the very depths of your soul and spirit. So be it.

ASSERTION # 9

We are now calling on the infinite, eternal power and help of God, Jesus Christ, the Holy Ghost and with unwavering faith, gratitude, humility, and unconditional love for them and they for you, and with their great healing power, and your sincere, heartfelt prayers, and their approval they will now help you release and expunge the desire within you that holds you captive and prevents you from attaining the healthy weight that you wish to attain. You will not select or support any diet that will harm you in any way. You will be very prudent in your selection of foods, and you will continually maintain the selected diet until the desired weight has been attained. You will completely accept this noble assertion from now on, which will penetrate to the very depths of your soul and spirit. So be it.

ASSERTION # 10

We are now calling on the infinite, eternal power and help of God, Jesus Christ, the Holy Ghost, and with unwavering faith, gratitude, humility, and unconditional love for them and they for you, with their great healing power, and your sincere, heartfelt prayers, and their approval they will now help you release and expunge the negative power within you that holds you captive to pain and illness. You will now release and expunge this evil power forever and you will now accept and execute this noble assertion from now on and forever. You are now definitely determined to honor this affirmation, which will penetrate to the very depths of your soul and spirit. so be it.

ASSERTION # 11

We are now calling on the infinite power and eternal help of God, Jesus Christ, the Holy Ghost, with unwavering faith, Gratitude, humility and unconditional love for them and they for you, and with their great healing power, and your sincere, heartfelt prayers, and their approval they will now help you rid yourself of the destructive influence of fear, which has adversely affected your life. You will now definitely forgive your () and yourself of this fear and act on this crucial choice from this moment on and forever. [() Indicates the source e.g. mother, father siblings etc.} With great determination you will honor this assertion, which will penetrate to he very depths of your soul and spirit. So be it.

ASSERTION # 12

We are now calling on the infinite power and eternal help of God, Jesus Christ, the Holy Ghost, and with their great healing power, and your unwavering faith, gratitude, humility, and unconditional love for them and they for you, and with your sincere, heartfelt prayers and their approval they will now help you rid yourself of the destructive element of pain, which had adversely affected your life. You will now definitely forgive your () and yourself of this fear and act on this crucial choice from this moment on and forever. You will now definitely honor this assertion, which will penetrate to your very soul and spirit. So be it.

ASSERTION # 13

We are now calling on the infinite power and eternal help of God, Jesus Christ, the Holy Ghost, and with unwavering faith, gratitude, humility and unconditional love for them and they for you, and with their great healing power, and your sincere, heartfelt prayers and their approval they will now help you rid yourself of the destructive element of shame, which has adversely affected your life. You will now definitely forgive your () and yourself of this shame and act on this crucial assertion from this moment on and forever. You will now definitely honor this assertion, which will penetrate to the very depths of your soul and spirit. So be it.

ASSERTION # 14

We are now calling on the infinite power and eternal help of God, Jesus Christ, the Holy Ghost, and with unwavering faith, gratitude, humility, and unconditional love for them and they for you, and with their great healing power and your sincere, heartfelt prayers and their approval they will now help you rid yourself of the destructive element of anger, which has adversely affected your life. You will now definitely forgive your () and yourself of this anger and act on this crucial assertion from this moment on and forever. You will now definitely honor this great assertion, which will penetrate to the very depths of your soul and spirit. So be it.

ASSERTION # 15

We are now calling on the infinite power and eternal help of God, Jesus Christ, the Holy Ghost, and with unwavering faith, humility, gratitude, and unconditional love for them and they for you, and with their great healing power, and your sincere, heartfelt prayers and their approval they will now help you rid yourself of the destructive element of guilt. You will now definitely forgive your () and yourself of this guilt, through repentance and act on this crucial choice from this moment on and forever. You will now definitely honor this great assertion, which will penetrate to the very depths of your soul and spirit. So be it.

ASSERTION # 16

We are now calling on the infinite power and eternal help of God, Jesus Christ, the Holy Ghost, and with unwavering faith, gratitude, humility, and unconditional love for them and they for you, and with their great healing power, and your sincere, heartfelt prayers and their approval they will now help you rid yourself of the destructive problem of holding grudges, which has adversely affected your life. You will now definitely forgive your () and yourself of holding grudges and act on this crucial choice from this moment on and forever. You will now definitely honor this assertion, which will penetrate to the very depths of your soul and spirit. So be it.

ASSERTION # 17

We are now calling on the infinite power and eternal help of God, Jesus Christ, the Holy Ghost, and with unwavering faith, gratitude, humility, and unconditional love for them and they for you, and with their great healing power, and your sincere, heartfelt prayers and their approval they will now help you rid yourself of the destructive element of resentment, which has adversely affected your life. You will now definitely forgive your () and yourself of this resentment, and act on this crucial choice from this moment on and forever. You will now gladly honor this assertion, which will penetrate to the very depths of your soul and spirit. So be it

ASSERTION # 18

We are now calling on the infinite power and eternal help of God, Jesus Christ, The Holy Ghost, and with unwavering faith, gratitude, humility, and unconditional love for them and they for you, and with their great healing power and your sincere, heartfelt prayers and their approval They will now help you rid yourself of the destructive element of hate, which has adversely affected your life. You will now definitely forgive your () and yourself of this hate and act on this crucial choice from this moment on and forever. You will now gladly honor this assertion, which will penetrate to the very depths of your soul and spirit. So be it

ASSERTION # 19

We are now calling on the infinite power and eternal help of God, Jesus Christ, the Holy Ghost, and with unwavering faith, gratitude, and unconditional love for them and they for you, and with their great healing power, and your sincere, heartfelt prayers, and their approval, They will now help you rid yourself of the destructive element of un-forgiveness, which has adversely affected your life. You will now definitely forgive your () and yourself of all un-forgiveness and act on this crucial choice from this moment on and forever. You will now gladly honor this assertion, which will penetrate to the very depths of your soul and spirit. So be it.

The following assertions/suggestions are designed to help the client overcome, some of the unrighteous elements, of traits and characteristics.

ASSERTION # 20

We are now calling on the infinite power and eternal help of God, Jesus Christ, the Holy Ghost, and with unwavering faith, gratitude, humility, and unconditional love for them and they for you, and with their great healing powers, and your sincere, prayers, and their approval, and upon your prayerful request, they will now help you rid yourself of the destructive element of anger. Anger is the basis for many of our problems. It is through anger that all contention begins. Anger is used to subdue others, to blackmail them, to force them to accept your opinions, whether they are right or wrong. Anger is one of the major tools of Satan. He uses it to diminish our right to choose, and use our agency. Anger can lead to rage from which many terrible events can occur, such as murder, rape, genocide and even whole countries have been known to fall because of it. So you will now definitely forgive yourself of all the uncontrolled episodes of anger that have occurred in your life. This is your commitment from this moment on and forever. You will now honor this assertion, which will penetrate to the very depths of your soul and spirit. So be it.

ASSERTION # 21

We are now calling on the infinite power and eternal help of God, Jesus Christ, the Holy Ghost, and with unwavering faith, gratitude, humility, and unconditional love for them and they for you, and with their great healing powers, and your sincere, heartfelt prayers, and their approval, and upon your prayerful request, they will now help you rid yourself of the destructive element of apathy. You will now definitely forgive yourself of all the times you have been apathetic in your life. This is your commitment from this moment on and forever. You will definitely honor this assertion, which will penetrate to the very depths of your soul and spirit. So be it.

ASSERTION # 22

We are now calling on the infinite power and eternal help of God, Jesus Christ, the Holy Ghost, and with unwavering faith, gratitude, humility and unconditional love for them and they for you, and with their great healing powers, and your sincere, heartfelt prayers, and their approval, and upon your prayerful request, they will now help you rid yourself of the destructive element of avarice. You will now definitely forgive yourself of all of the times you have expressed avarice. This is your commitment from this moment on and forever. You will now definitely honor this assertion, which will penetrate to the very depths of your soul and spirit. So be it.

ASSERTION # 23

We are now calling on the infinite power and eternal help of God, Jesus Christ, the Holy Ghost, and with unwavering faith, gratitude, humility, and unconditional love for them and they for you, and with their great healing powers, and your sincere, heartfelt prayers, and their approval, and upon your prayerful request, they will now help you rid yourself of the destructive element of callousness. You will now definitely forgive yourself of every time you have been callous and uncaring. This is your commitment from this moment on and forever. You will definitely honor this assertion, which will penetrate to the very depths of your soul and spirit. So be it.

ASSERTION # 24

We are now calling on the infinite power and eternal help of God, Jesus Christ, The Holy Ghost, and with unwavering faith, humility, gratitude, and unconditional love for them and they for you, and with their great healing powers, and your sincere, heartfelt prayers and their approval, and upon your prayerful request, they will now help you rid yourself of the destructive element of cheating. You will now definitely forgive yourself of every time you have cheated on others and yourself. This is your commitment from this moment on and forever. You will definitely honor this assertion, which will penetrate to the very depths of your soul and spirit. So be it.

ASSERTION # 25

We are now calling on the infinite power and eternal help of God, Jesus Christ, the Holy Ghost, and with unwavering faith, humility, gratitude, and unconditional love for them and they for you, and with their great healing powers and your sincere, heartfelt prayers and their approval, and upon your prayerful request, they will now help you rid yourself of the destructive element of contempt. You will now definitely forgive yourself for every time you have demonstrated contempt for anyone. This is your commitment from this moment on and forever. You will definitely honor this assertion, which will penetrate to the very depths of your soul and spirit. So be it.

ASSERTION # 26

We are now calling on the infinite power and eternal help of God, Jesus Christ, the Holy Ghost, and with unwavering faith, humility, gratitude, and unconditional love for them and they for you, and with their great healing powers, and your sincere, heartfelt prayers and their approval, and upon your prayerful request, they will now help you rid yourself of the destructive element of contention. You will now definitely forgive yourself for all of the times you have created a condition of contention in some ones life. This is your commitment from this moment on and forever. You will definitely honor this assertion, which will penetrate to the very depths of your soul and spirit. So be it.

ASSERTION # 27

We are now calling on the infinite power and eternal help of God, Jesus Christ, the Holy Ghost, and with unwavering faith, humility, Gratitude, and unconditional love for them and they for you, and with their great healing posers, and your sincere, heartfelt prayers and their approval, and upon your prayerful request, they will now help you rid yourself of the destructive problem of being controlling. You will now definitely forgive yourself for all of the times you have exercised unrighteous control over any one. This is your commitment from this moment on and forever. You will definitely honor this assertion, which will penetrate to the very depths of your soul and spirit. So be it.

ASSERTION # 28

We are now calling on the infinite power and eternal help of God, Jesus Christ, the Holy Ghost, and with unwavering faith, humility, Gratitude, and unconditional love for them and they for you, and with their great healing powers, and your sincere, heartfelt prayers and their approval, and upon your prayerful request, they will now help you rid yourself of the destructive element of cowardice. You will now definitely forgive yourself for every time you have shown cowardice. Instead of cowardice you will demonstrate courage from this moment on and forever. You will definitely honor this assertion, which will penetrate to the very depths of your soul and spirit. So be it.

ASSERTION # 29

We are now calling on the infinite power and eternal help of God, Jesus Christ, the Holy Ghost, and with unwavering faith, humility, gratitude, and unconditional love for them and they for you, and with their great healing powers, and your sincere, heartfelt prayers and their approval, and upon your prayerful request, they will now help you rid yourself of the destructive element of cruelty. You will now definitely forgive yourself for all of the times you have demonstrated cruelty to anyone or anything. This is your commitment from this moment on and forever. You will now definitely honor this assertion, which will penetrate to the very depths of your soul and spirit. So be it.

ASSERTION # 30

We are now calling on the infinite power and eternal help of God, Jesus Christ, the Holy Ghost, and with unwavering faith, gratitude, and unconditional love for them and they for you, and with their great healing powers, and your sincere, heartfelt prayers and their approval, and upon your prayerful request, they will now help you rid you of the destructive practice of denying responsibility for all of your actions. You will now definitely forgive yourself for all of the times you have denied responsibility for your actions. This is your commitment from this moment on and forever. You will now definitely honor this assertion, which will penetrate to the very depths of your soul and spirit. So be it.

ASSERTION # 31

We are now calling on the infinite power and eternal help of God, Jesus Christ, the Holy Ghost, and with unwavering faith, humility, gratitude, and unconditional love for them and they for you, and with their great healing powers, and your sincere, heartfelt prayers and their approval, and upon your prayerful request, they will now choose to help you rid yourself of the destructive problem of being devilish and evil. You will now definitely forgive yourself for all of the events, in which you were involved with evil acts. This is your commitment from this moment on and forever. You will now honestly honor this assertion, which will penetrate to the very depths of your soul and spirit. So be it.

ASSERTION # 32

We are now calling on the infinite power and eternal help of God, Jesus Christ, the Holy Ghost, and with unwavering faith, humility, gratitude, and unconditional love for them and they for you, and with their great healing powers, and your sincere, heartfelt prayers and their approval, and upon your prayerful request, they will now help you rid yourself of the destructive element of dishonesty. You will now definitely forgive yourself for all of the events, in which you were dishonest. This is your commitment from this moment on and forever. You will now definitely honor this assertion, which will penetrate to the very depths of your soul and spirit. So be it.

ASSERTION # 33

We are now calling on the infinite power and eternal help of God, Jesus Christ, the Holy Ghost, and with unwavering faith, humility, gratitude, and unconditional love for them and they for you, and with their great healings powers, and your sincere, heartfelt prayers and their approval, and upon your prayerful request, they will now help you rid yourself of the destructive practice of being disloyal to God, close relatives and friends. You will always put God first in the order of loyalties. This is your commitment from this moment on and forever. You will now definitely honor this assertion, which will penetrate to the very depths of your soul and spirit. So be it.

ASSERTION # 34

We are now calling on the infinite power and eternal help of God, Jesus Christ, the Holy Ghost, and with unwavering faith, humility, gratitude, and unconditional love for them and they for you, and with their great healing powers, and your sincere, heartfelt prayers, and their approval, and upon your prayerful request, they will now help you rid yourself of the destructive practice of being disobedient to God's commandments. You will now forgive yourself, and ask God's forgiveness for all of the times you have been disobedient. This is your commitment from this moment on and forever. You will now definitely honor this assertion, which will penetrate to the very depths of your soul and spirit. So be it.

ASSERTION # 35

We are now calling on the infinite power and eternal help of God, Jesus Christ, the Holy Ghost, and with unwavering faith, humility, gratitude, and unconditional love for them and they for you, and with their great healing powers, and your sincere, heartfelt prayers, and their approval, and upon your prayerful request, they will now help you rid yourself of the destructive habit of being disorderly and disorganized. You will now forgive yourself of being disorganized and disorderly. You will now be neat in all situations and events. This is your commitment from this moment on and forever. You will now definitely honor this assertion, which will penetrate to the very depths of your soul and spirit. So be it.

ASSERTION # 36

We are now calling on the infinite power and eternal help of God, Jesus Christ, the Holy Ghost, and with unwavering faith, humility, gratitude, and unconditional love for them and they for you, and with their great healing powers and your sincere, heartfelt prayers, and their approval, and upon your prayerful request, they will now help you rid yourself of the destructive element of doubt. You will now forgive yourself for all of the events and situations in which you have felt doubt. This is your commitment from this moment on and forever. You will now definitely honor this assertion, which will penetrate to the very depths of your soul and spirit. So be it.

ASSERTION # 37

We are now calling on the infinite power and eternal help of God, Jesus Christ, the Holy Ghost, and with unwavering faith, humility, gratitude, and unconditional love for them and they for you, and with their great healing powers, and your sincere, heartfelt prayers, and their approval, and upon your prayerful request, they will now help you rid yourself of the destructive element of egotism. You will now forgive yourself for displaying egotism, and pride, wherever you go. This is your commitment from this moment on and forever. You will now definitely honor this assertion, which will penetrate to the very depths of your soul and spirit. So be it.

ASSERTION # 38

We are now calling on the infinite power and eternal help of God, Jesus Christ, the Holy Ghost, and with unwavering faith, humility, gratitude, and unconditional love for them and they for you, and with their great healing powers, and your sincere, heartfelt prayers, and their approval, and upon your prayerful request, they will now help you rid yourself of the destructive element of envy. You will now forgive yourself of any time you have to been envious in your life. This is your commitment from this moment on and forever. You will now definitely honor this assertion, which will penetrate to the very depths of your soul and spirit. So be it

ASSERTION # 39

We are now calling on the infinite power and eternal help of God, Jesus Christ, the Holy Ghost, and with absolute faith, gratitude, and unconditional love for them and they for you, and with their great healing powers, and your sincere, heartfelt prayers, and their approval, and upon your prayerful request, they will now help you rid yourself of the destructive habit of gossiping. You will now forgive yourself of all of the times you have gossiped, and lied about someone. This is your commitment from this moment on and forever. You will now definitely honor this assertion, which will penetrate to the very depths of your soul and spirit. So be it.

ASSERTION # 40

We are now calling on the infinite power and eternal help of God, Jesus Christ, the Holy Ghost, and with unwavering faith, humility, gratitude, and unconditional love for them and they for you, and with their great healing powers, and your sincere, heartfelt prayers, and their approval, and upon your prayerful request, they will now help you rid yourself of the destructive element of Greed. You will now forgive yourself of all of the times you have been greedy. This is your commitment from this moment on and forever. You will now definitely honor this assertion, which will penetrate to the very depths of your soul and spirit. So be it.

ASSERTION # 41

We are now calling on the infinite power and eternal help of God, Jesus Christ, the Holy Ghost, and with unwavering faith, humility, gratitude, and unconditional love for them and they for you, and with their great healing powers, and your sincere, heartfelt prayers, and their approval, and upon your prayerful request, they will now help you rid yourself of the destructive element of hostility. You will now forgive yourself of whenever you have been, or could be, hostile towards anyone. This is your commitment from this moment on. You will now definitely honor this assertion, which will penetrate to the very depths of your soul and spirit. So be it.

ASSERTION # 42

We are now calling on the infinite power and eternal help of God, Jesus Christ, the Holy Ghost, and with unwavering faith, humility, Gratitude, and unconditional love for them and they for you, and with their great healing powers and your sincere, heartfelt prayers, and their approval, and upon your prayerful request, they will now help you rid yourself of the destructive practice of being hardhearted. You will now forgive yourself of ever being, or could be, hardhearted. This is your commitment from this moment on and forever. You will now definitely honor this assertion, which will penetrate to the very depths of your soul and spirit. So be it.

ASSERTION # 43

We are now calling on the infinite power and eternal help of God, Jesus Christ, the Holy Ghost, and with unwavering faith, humility, gratitude, and unconditional love for them and they for you, and with their great healing powers and your sincere, heartfelt prayers, and their approval, and upon your prayerful request, they will now help you rid yourself of the destructive practice of being hatful. You will now forgive yourself of all of the times in your life you have felt hate for someone. Hate is no longer a part of your personality. This is your commitment from this moment on and forever. You will now definitely honor this assertion, which will penetrate to the very depths of your soul and spirit. So be it.

ASSERTION # 44

We are now calling on the infinite power and eternal help of God, Jesus Christ, the Holy Ghost, and with unwavering faith, humility, gratitude, and unconditional love for them and they for you, and with their great healing powers, and your sincere, heartfelt prayers, and their approval, and upon your prayerful request, they will now help you rid yourself of the destructive practice of be of being intolerant. You will now forgive yourself of all of the times in your life you have been, or could be, intolerant of someone. This is your commitment from this moment on and forever. You will definitely honor this assertion, which will penetrate to the very depths of your soul and sprit. So be it.

ASSERTION # 45

We are now calling on the infinite power and eternal help of God, Jesus Christ, the Holy Ghost, and with unwavering faith, humility, gratitude, and unconditional love for them and they for you, and with their great healing powers, and your sincere, heartfelt prayers, and their approval, and upon your prayerful request, they will now help you rid yourself of the evil practice of being irreverent. You will now be reverent at all appropriate times in your life. This is your commitment from this moment on and forever. You will now definitely honor this assertion, which will penetrate to the very depths of your soul and spirit. So be it.

ASSERTION # 46

We are now calling on the infinite power and eternal help of God, Jesus Christ, the Holy Ghost, and with unwavering faith, humility, gratitude, and unconditional love for them and they for you, and with their great healing powers and your sincere, heartfelt prayers, and their approval, and upon your prayerful request, they will now help you rid yourself of the practice of being irresponsible. You will now be very responsible for your every act. This is your commitment from this moment on and forever. You will now definitely honor this assertion, which will penetrate to thee very depths of your soul and spirit. So be it.

ASSERTION # 47

We are now calling on the infinite power and eternal help of God, Jesus Christ, the Holy Ghost, and with unwavering faith, humility, gratitude, and unconditional love for them and they for you, and with their great healing powers, and your sincere, heartfelt prayers, and their approval, and upon your prayerful request, they will now help you rid yourself of the practice of being insincere. You will now forgive yourself of ever being insincere in your relationship with others. This is your commitment from this moment on and forever. You will definitely honor this assertion, which will penetrate to the very depth of your soul and spirit. So be it.

ASSERTION # 48

We are now calling on the infinite power and eternal help of God, Jesus Christ, the Holy Ghost, and with unwavering faith, humility, gratitude, and unconditional love for them and they for you, and with their great healing powers, and your sincere, heartfelt prayers, and their approval, and upon your prayerful request, they will now help you rid yourself of the evil of being jealous of anyone for anything. You will now forgive yourself of ever being jealous of anyone. This is your commitment from this moment on and forever. You will now definitely honor this assertion, which will penetrate to the very depth of your soul and spirit. So be it.

ASSERTION # 49

We are now calling on the infinite power and eternal help of God, Jesus Christ, the Holy Ghost, and with unwavering faith, humility, gratitude, and unconditional love for them and they for you, and with their great healing powers, and your sincere, heartfelt prayers, and their approval, and upon your prayerful request, they will now help you rid yourself of the endless practice of being lazy. You will now forgive yourself of the terrible habit of being lazy. Your desire to get things done will be one of the top priorities in your life. This is your commitment from this moment on and forever. You will now definitely honor this assertion, which will penetrate to the very depths of your soul and spirit. So be it,

ASSERTION # 50

We are now calling on the infinite power and eternal help of God, Jesus Christ, the Holy Ghost, and with unwavering faith, humility, gratitude, and unconditional love for them and they for you, and with their great healing powers, and your sincere, heartfelt prayers, and their approval, and upon your prayerful request, they will now help you rid yourself of the evil habit of lying. You will now forgive yourself of this terrible habit. This is your commitment from this moment on and forever. You will now definitely honor this assertion, which will penetrate to the very depths of your soul and spirit. So be it.

ASSERTION # 51

We are now calling on the infinite power and eternal help of God, Jesus Christ, the Holy Ghost, and with unwavering faith, humility, gratitude, unconditional love for them and they for you, and with their great healing powers, and your sincere, heartfelt prayers, and their approval, and upon your prayerful request, they will now help you rid yourself of the evil of lusting after that which is forbidden. You will now forgive yourself of ever being lustful. This is your commitment from this moment on and forever. You will now definitely honor this assertion, which will penetrate to the very depths of your soul and spirit. So be it.

ASSERTION # 52

We are now calling on the infinite power and eternal help of God, Jesus Christ, the Holy Ghost, and with unwavering faith, humility, gratitude, unconditional love for them and they for you, and with their great healing powers, and your sincere, heartfelt prayers, and their approval, and upon your prayerful request, they will now help you rid yourself of the evil of malevolence. You will now forgive yourself of being malevolent toward any one. This is your commitment from this moment on and forever. You will now definitely honor this assertion, which will penetrate to the very depths of your soul and spirit. So be it.

ASSERTION # 53

We are now calling on the infinite power and eternal help of God, Jesus Christ, the Holy Ghost, and with unwavering faith, humility, gratitude, unconditional love for them and they for you, and with their great healing powers, and your sincere, heartfelt prayers, and your approval, and upon your prayerful request, they will now help you rid yourself of the evil of malice. You will now forgive yourself of the many times you have had malice towards others. This is your commitment from this moment on and forever. You will now definitely honor this assertion, which will penetrate to the very depths of your soul and spirit. So be it.

ASSERTION # 54

We are now calling on the infinite power and eternal help of God, Jesus Christ, the Holy Ghost, and with unwavering faith, humility, gratitude, unconditional love for them and they for you, and with their great healing powers, and your sincere, heartfelt prayers, and their approval, and upon your prayerful request, they will now help you rid yourself of being mean to others. You will now forgive yourself of the many times you have been mean to those you love and to others. This is your commitment from this moment on and forever. You will now definitely honor this assertion, which will penetrate to the very depths of your soul and spirit. So be it.

ASSERTION # 55

We are now calling on the infinite power and eternal help of God, Jesus Christ, the Holy Ghost, and with unwavering faith, humility, gratitude, unconditional love for them and they for you, and with their great healing powers, and your sincere, heartfelt prayers, and their approval, and upon your prayerful request, they will now help you rid yourself of not being merciful to those you love and to all others. You will now forgive yourself of not showing mercy to those who have trespassed against you. This is your commitment from this moment on and forever. You will now definitely honor this assertion, which will penetrate to the very depths of your soul and spirit. So be it.

ASSERTION # 56

We are now calling on the infinite power and eternal help of God, Jesus Christ, the Holy Ghost, and with unwavering faith, humility, gratitude, unconditional love for them and they for you, and with their great healing powers, and your sincere, heartfelt prayers, and their approval, and upon your prayerful request, they will now help you rid yourself of not repenting of your sins, indiscretions and imperfections. You will now forgive yourself of not being repentant. You will now repent on a daily basis. This is your commitment from this moment on and forever. This assertion will penetrate to the very depths of your soul and spirit. So be it.

ASSERTION # 57

We are now calling on the infinite power and eternal help of God, Jesus Christ, the Holy Ghost, and with unwavering faith, humility, gratitude, unconditional love for them and they for you, and with their great healing powers, and your sincere, heartfelt prayers, and their approval, and upon your prayerful request, they will now help you rid yourself of the habit of polluting your surroundings. You will now forgive yourself of this bad habit. This is your commitment from this moment on and forever. You will definitely honor this assertion, which will penetrate to the very depths of your soul and spirit. So be it.

ASSERTION # 58

We are now calling on the infinite power and eternal help of God, Jesus Christ, the Holy Ghost, and with unwavering faith, humility, gratitude, unconditional love for them and they for you, and with their great healing powers, and your sincere, heartfelt prayers, and their approval, and upon your prayerful request, they will now help you rid yourself of being prejudiced against anyone for anything. You will now forgive yourself of all facets of prejudice in any form. This is your commitment from this moment on and forever. You will now definitely honor this assertion, which will penetrate to the very depths of your soul and spirit. So be it.

ASERTION # 59

We are now calling on the infinite power and eternal help of God, Jesus Christ, the Holy Ghost, and with unwavering faith, humility, gratitude, unconditional love for them and they for you, and with their great healing powers, and your sincere, heartfelt prayers, and their approval, and upon your prayerful request, they will now help you rid yourself of your prideful feelings for things you have desired and events involving those you love and care for. You will now forgive yourself of the destructive element of pride. This is your commitment from this moment on and forever. You will definitely honor this assertion, which will penetrate to the very depths of your soul and spirit. So be it.

ASSERTION # 60

We are now calling on the infinite power and eternal help of God, Jesus Christ, the Holy Ghost, and with unwavering faith, humility, gratitude, unconditional love for them and they for you, and with their great healing powers, and your sincere, heartfelt prayers, and their approval and upon your prayerful request, they will now help you rid yourself of the terrible practice of seeking revenge when someone has offended you. "Vengeance is mine saith the Lord, and I will repay." (Rom. 12:19) You will now forgive yourself of this terrible practice. This is your commitment from this moment on and forever. Your desire now is to honor this, assertion, which will penetrate to the very depths of your soul and spirit. so be it.

ASSERTION # 61

We are now calling on the infinite power and eternal help of God, Jesus Christ, the Holy Ghost, and with unwavering faith, humility, gratitude, unconditional love for them and they for you, and with their great healing powers, and your sincere, heartfelt prayers, and their approval, and upon your prayerful request, they will now help you rid yourself of the practice of being selfish. You will now forgive yourself of every time you have been selfish. This is your commitment from this moment on and forever. Your desire now is to honor this assertion, which will penetrate to the very depths of your soul and spirit. So be it.

ASSERTION # 62

We are now calling on the infinite power and eternal help of God, Jesus Christ, the Holy Ghost, and with unwavering faith, humility, gratitude, unconditional love for them and they for you, and with their great healing posers, and your sincere, heartfelt prayers, and with their approval, and upon your prayerful request, they will now help you rid yourself of the practice of being slothful. You will now forgive yourself of your slothfulness and display the elements of neatness and cleanliness. This is your commitment from this moment on and forever. Your desire now is to honor this assertion, which will penetrate to the very depths of your soul and spirit. So be it.

ASSERTION # 63

We are now calling on the infinite power and eternal help of God, Jesus Christ, the Holy Ghost, and with unwavering faith, humility, gratitude, unconditional love for them and they for you, and with their great healing powers, and your sincere, heartfelt prayers, and their approval, and upon your prayerful request, they will now help you rid yourself of being tactless. You will now forgive yourself of being tactless for your lifetime. This is your commitment from this moment on and forever. Your desire now is to honor this assertion, which will penetrate to the very depths of your soul and spirit. So be it.

ASSERTION # 64

We are now calling on the infinite power and eternal help of God, Jesus Christ, the Holy Ghost, and with unwavering faith, humility, gratitude, unconditional love for them and they for you, and with their great healing powers, and your sincere, heartfelt prayers, and their approval, and upon your prayerful request, they will now help you rid yourself of being thankless. You will now forgive yourself for not giving thanks, to Deity and everyone with whom you come in contact. This is your commitment from this moment on and forever. Your desire now is to honor this assertion, which will penetrate to the very depths of your soul and your spirit. So be it.

ASSERTION # 65

We are now calling on the infinite power and eternal help of God, Jesus Christ, the Holy Ghost, and with unwavering faith, humility, gratitude, unconditional love for them and they for you, and with their great healing powers, and your sincere, heartfelt prayers, and their approval, and upon your prayerful request, they will now help you rid yourself of being thoughtless. Being thoughtless really is being uncaring. You will now forgive yourself for being thoughtless and uncaring for those you love and for everyone. This is your commitment from this moment on and forever. Your desire now is to honor this assertion, which will penetrate to the very depths of your soul and spirit. So be it.

ASSERTION # 66

We are now calling on the infinite power and eternal help of God, Jesus Christ, the Holy Ghost, and with unwavering faith, humility, gratitude, unconditional love for them and they for you, and with their great healing powers, and your sincere, heartfelt prayers, and their approval, and upon your prayerful request, they will now help you rid yourself of not being chaste. Chastity is one of the traits that should be cherished and protected at all costs. Once lost, it can never be regained, but it can be forgiven. You will now repent of being unchaste. Protect your chastity from this moment on and forever. Your desire now is to honor this assertion, which will penetrate to the very depths of your soul and spirit. So be it.

ASSERTION # 67

We are now calling on the infinite power and eternal help of God, Jesus Christ, the Holy Ghost, and with unwavering faith, humility, gratitude, unconditional love for them and they for you, and with their great healing power, and your sincere, heartfelt prayers, and their approval, and upon your prayerful request, they will now help you rid yourself of being undisciplined. Without discipline little could be accomplished. You will now put a high priority on being disciplined. This is your commitment from this moment on and forever. Your desire now is to honor this assertion, which will penetrate to the very depths of your soul and spirit. So be it.

ASSERTION # 68

We are now calling on the infinite power and eternal help of God, Jesus Christ, the Holy Ghost, and with unwavering faith, humility, gratitude, unconditional love for them and they for you, and with their great healing powers and your sincere, heartfelt prayers, and their approval, and upon your prayerful request, they will now help you rid yourself of un-forgiveness. You will now forgive yourself for every un-forgiveness act you have carried throughout your life. This is your commitment from this moment on and forever. Your desire now is to honor this assertion, which will penetrate to the very depths of your soul and spirit. So be it.

ASSERTION # 69

We are now calling on the infinite power and eternal help of God, Jesus Christ, the Holy Ghost, and with unwavering faith, humility, gratitude, unconditional love for them and they for you, and with their great healing powers, and your sincere, heartfelt prayers, and their approval, and upon your prayerful request, they will now help you rid yourself of being unlawful. You should not only obey man's laws but God's laws as well. You will now forgive yourself of being unlawful. This is your commitment from this moment on and forever. Your desire now is to honor this assertion, which will penetrate to the very depths of your soul and spirit. So be it.

ASSERTION # 70

We are now calling on the infinite power and eternal help of God, Jesus Christ, the Holy Ghost, and with unwavering faith, humility, gratitude, unconditional love for them and they for you, and with their great healing powers, and your sincere, heartfelt prayers, and their approval, and upon your prayerful request, they will now help you rid yourself of not being prayerful in all of your activities and accomplishments. You will now forgive yourself of not being diligent in your prayerfulness. Pray always. This is your commitment from this moment on and forever. You are now determined to honor this assertion, which will penetrate to the very depths of your soul and spirit. So be it.

ASSERTION # 71

We are now calling on the infinite power and eternal help of God, Jesus Christ, the Holy Ghost, and with unwavering faith, humility, gratitude, unconditional love for them and they for you, and with their great healing powers, and your sincere, heartfelt prayers, and their approval, and upon your prayerful request, they will now help you rid yourself of not being trustworthy. You will now forgive yourself of all of the times you have been untrustworthy. This is your commitment from this moment on and forever. You are now determined to honor this assertion, which will penetrate to the very depths of your soul and spirit. So be it.

Chapter Six

ASSERTIONS OF THE RIGHTEOUS ELEMENTS OF LOVE

THE PATH TO PERFECTION REQUIRES us to embrace the elements of righteousness and love and maximize their perfection by increasing their effectiveness in our lives.

There are approximately two hundred of these elements of which I have chosen approximately seventy-five. These are the ones that, for me, are the most important. If there are others, which are more important to you, add them to this list using the same basic format.

Be sure you choose a partner (voice) that is sensitive to your needs, and who will be motivated enough to maximize each unit so it's effectiveness will fill your needs.

ASSERTION # 1

We are now calling on the infinite power and eternal help of God, Jesus Christ, the Holy Ghost and with absolute faith, gratitude, and unconditional love for them and they for you, and with their great healing power, and your sincere, heartfelt supplications, and their approval, and upon your prayerful request, they will now help you embrace and perfect the righteous element of appreciation. You will no longer procrastinate in perfecting this element. With determination and irreversible will power, you will now positively act on this decision from this moment on and forever. You will definitely honor this assertion, which will penetrate to the very depths of your soul and spirit. So be it.

ASSERTION # 2

We are now calling on the infinite, power and eternal help of God, Jesus Christ, the Holy Ghost, and with absolute faith, gratitude, and unconditional love for them and they for you, and with their great healing power, and your sincere, heartfelt supplications, and their approval, and upon your prayerful request they will now help you embrace and perfect the righteous element of benevolence. With determination and irreversible willpower, you will now positively act on this decision from this moment on and forever. You will definitely honor this assertion, which will penetrate to the very depths of your soul and spirit. So be it.

ASSERTION # 3

We are now calling on the infinite, power and eternal help of God, Jesus Christ, the Holy Ghost, and with absolute faith, gratitude, unconditional love for them and they for you, and with their great healing power, and your sincere, heartfelt supplication sand their ,approval, and upon your prayerful request they will now help you embrace and perfect the righteous element of charity, which is the pure love of Christ. With determination and irreversible willpower you will now positively act on this decision from this moment on and forever. You will definitely honor this assertion, which will penetrate to the very depths of your soul and spirit. So be it.

ASSERTION # 4

We are now calling on the infinite, power and eternal help of God, Jesus Christ, the Holy Ghost, and with absolute faith, gratitude, unconditional love for them and they for you, and with their great healing power, and your sincere, heartfelt supplications, and their approval, and upon your prayerful request, they will now help you embrace and perfect the righteous element of cleanliness. With determination and irreversible willpower, you will now positively act on this decision from this moment on and forever. You will definitely honor this assertion, which will penetrate to the very depths of your soul and spirit. So be it.

ASSERTIOIN # 5

We are now calling on the infinite power and eternal help of God, Jesus Christ, the Holy Ghost, and with absolute faith, Gratitude, unconditional love for them and they for you, and with their great healing powers, and your sincere, heartfelt supplications, and their approval, and upon your prayerful request, they will now help you embrace and perfect the righteous element of compassion. With determination and irreversible willpower, you will now positively act on this decision from this moment on and forever. You will definitely honor this assertion, which will penetrate to the very depths of your soul and spirit. So be it.

ASSERTION # 6

We are now calling on the infinite power and eternal help of God, Jesus Christ, the Holy Ghost, and with absolute faith, gratitude, unconditional love for them and they for you, and with their great healing powers, and your sincere, heartfelt supplications, and their approval, and upon your prayerful request, they will now help you embrace and perfect the righteous element of confidence. With determination and irreversible willpower, you will now positively act on this decision from this moment on and forever. You are determined to honor this assertion, which will penetrate to the very depths of your soul and spirit. So be it.

ASSERTION # 7

We are now calling on the infinite power and eternal help of God, Jesus Christ, the Holy Ghost, and with absolute faith, gratitude, unconditional love for them and they for you, and with their great healing powers, and your sincere, heartfelt supplications, and their approval, and upon your prayerful request, they will now help you embrace and perfect the righteous element of courage. With determination and irreversible willpower, you will now positively act on this decision from this moment on and forever. You will now definitely honor this assertion, which will penetrate to the very depths of your soul and spirit. So be it.

ASSERTION # 8

We are now calling on the infinite power and eternal help of God, Jesus Christ, the Holy Ghost, and with absolute faith, gratitude, unconditional love for them and they for you, and with their great healing powers, and your sincere, heartfelt supplications, and their approval, and upon your prayerful request, they will now help you embrace and perfect the righteous element of consideration. With determination and irreversible willpower, you will now positively act on this decision from this moment on and forever. You will now definitely honor this assertion, which will penetrate to the very depth of your soul and spirit. So be it,

ASSERTION # 9

We are now calling on the infinite power and eternal help of God, Jesus Christ, the Holy Ghost, and with absolute faith, gratitude, unconditional love for them and they for you, and with their great healing powers, and your sincere, heartfelt supplications, and their approval, and upon your prayerful request, they will now help you embrace and perfect the righteous element of creativity. With determination and irreversible willpower, you will now positively act on this decision from this moment on and forever. You will now definitely honor this assertion, which will penetrate to the very depths of your soul and spirit. So be it.

ASSERTION # 10

We are now calling on the infinite power and eternal help of God, Jesus Christ, the Holy Ghost, and with absolute faith, gratitude, unconditional love for them and they for you, and with their great healing powers, and your sincere, heartfelt supplication, and their approval, and upon your prayerful request, they will now help you embrace and perfect the righteous element of dedication. With determination and irreversible willpower, you will now positively act on this decision from this moment on and forever. With determination you will honor this assertion, which will penetrate to the very depths of your soul and spirit. So be it.

ASSERTION # 11

We are now calling on the infinite power and eternal help of God, Jesus Christ, the Holy Ghost, and with absolute faith, gratitude, unconditional love for them and they for you, and with their great healing powers, and your sincere heartfelt supplications, and their approval, and upon your prayerful request, they will now help you embrace and perfect the righteous element of discernment. With determination and irreversible willpower, you will now positively act on this decision from this moment on and forever. You are determined to honor this assertion, which will penetrate to the very soul and spirit. So be it.

ASSERTION # 12

We are now calling on the infinite power and eternal help of God, Jesus Christ, the Holy Ghost, and with absolute faith, gratitude, unconditional love for them and they for you, and with their great healing powers, and your sincere, heartfelt supplications, and their approval, and upon your prayerful request, they will now help you embrace and perfect the righteous element of durability. With determination and irreversible willpower, you will now positively act on this decision from this moment on and forever. You will now definitely honor this assertion, which will penetrate to the very depths of your soul and spirit. So be it.

ASSERTION # 13

We are now calling on the infinite power and eternal help of God, Jesus Christ, the Holy Ghost, and with absolute faith, gratitude, unconditional love for them and they for you, and with their great healing powers, and your sincere, heartfelt supplications, and their approval, and upon your prayerful request they will now help you embrace and perfect the righteous element of empathy. With determination and irreversible willpower, you will now positively act on this decision from this moment on and forever. You will now definitely honor this assertion, which will penetrate to the very depths of your soul and spirit. So be it.

ASSERTION # 14

We are now calling on the infinite power and eternal help of God, Jesus Christ, the Holy Ghost, and with absolute faith, gratitude, unconditional love for them and they for you, and with their great healing powers, and your sincere, heartfelt supplications, and their approval, and upon your prayerful request, they will now help you embrace and perfect the righteous element of equality. With determination and irreversible willpower, you will now positively act on this decision from this moment on and forever. You will now definitely honor this assertion, which will penetrate to the very depths of your soul and spirit. So be it.

ASSERTION # 15

We are now calling on the infinite power and eternal help of God, Jesus Christ, the Holy Ghost, and with absolute faith, gratitude, unconditional love for them and they for you, and with their great healing powers, and your sincere, heartfelt supplications, and their approval, and upon your prayerful request, they will now help you embrace and perfect the righteous element of faith. With determination and irreversible willpower, you will now positively act on this decision from this moment on and forever. You will now definitely honor this assertion, which will penetrate to the very depths of your soul and spirit. So be it.

ASSERTION # 16

We are now calling on the infinite power and eternal help of God, Jesus Christ, the Holy Ghost, and with absolute faith, Gratitude, unconditional love for them and they for you, and with their great healing powers, and your sincere, heartfelt supplications, and their approval, and upon your prayerful request, they will now help you embrace and perfect the righteous element of forgiveness. With determination and irreversible willpower, you will now positively act on this decision from this moment on and forever. You will now definitely honor this assertion, which will penetrate to the very depths of your soul and spirit. So be it.

ASSERTION # 17

We are now calling on the infinite power and eternal help of God, Jesus Christ, the Holy Ghost, and with absolute faith, gratitude, unconditional love for them and they for you, and with their great healing powers, and your sincere, heartfelt supplications, and their approval, and upon your prayerful request, they will now help you embrace and perfect the righteous element of friendliness. With determination and irreversible willpower, you will now positively act on this decision from this moment on and forever. You will now definitely honor this assertion, which will penetrate to the very depths of your soul and spirit. So be it.

ASSERTION # 18

We are now calling on the infinite power and eternal help of God, Jesus Christ, the Holy Ghost, and with absolute faith, gratitude, unconditional love for them and they for you, and with their great healing powers, and your sincere, heartfelt supplications, and their approval, and upon your prayerful request, they will now help you embrace and perfect the righteous element of being goal oriented. With determination and irreversible willpower, you will now positively act on this decision from this moment on and forever. You will now definitely honor this assertion, which will penetrate to the very depths of your soul and spirit. So be it.

ASSERTION # 19

We are now calling on the infinite power and eternal help of God, Jesus Christ, the Holy Ghost, and with absolute faith, gratitude, unconditional love for them and they for you, and with their great healing powers, and your sincere, heartfelt supplications, and their approval, and upon your prayerful request, they will now help you embrace and perfect the righteous element of gentleness. With determination and irreversible willpower, you will now positively act on this decision from this moment on and forever. You will now definitely honor this assertion, which will penetrate to the very depths of your soul and spirit. So be it.

ASSERTION # 20

We are now calling on the infinite power and eternal help of God, Jesus Christ, the Holy Ghost, and with absolute faith, gratitude, unconditional love for them and they for you, and with their great healing powers, and your sincere, heartfelt supplications, and their approval, and upon your prayerful request, they will now help you embrace and perfect the righteous element of being helpful. With determination and irreversible willpower, you will now positively act on this decision from this moment on and forever. You will now definitely honor this assertion, which will penetrate to the very depths of your soul and spirit. So be it.

ASSERTION # 21

We are now calling on the infinite power and eternal help of God, Jesus Christ, the Holy Ghost, and with absolute faith, gratitude, unconditional love for them and they for you, with their great healing powers, and your sincere, heartfelt supplications, and their approval, and upon your prayerful request they will now help you embrace and perfect the righteous element of honesty. With determination and irreversible willpower, you will now positively act on this decision from this moment on and forever. You will now definitely honor this assertion, which will penetrate to the very depths of your soul and spirit. So be it.

ASSERTION # 22

We are now calling on the infinite power and eternal help of God, Jesus Christ, the Holy Ghost, and with absolute faith, gratitude, unconditional love for them and they for you, and with their great healing powers, and your sincere, heartfelt supplications, and their approval, and upon your prayerful request, they will now help you embrace and perfect the righteous element of being honorable. With determination and irreversible willpower, you will now positively act on this decision from this moment on and forever. You will now definitely honor this assertion, which will penetrate to the very depths of your soul and spirit. So be it.

ASSERTION # 23

We are now calling on the infinite power and eternal help of God, Jesus Christ, the Holy Ghost, and with absolute faith, gratitude, unconditional love for them and they for you, and with their great healing powers, and your sincere, heartfelt supplications, and their approval, and upon your prayerful request, they will now help you embrace and perfect the righteous element of being hopeful. With determination and irreversible willpower, you will now positively act on this decision from this moment on and forever. You will now definitely honor this assertion, which will penetrate to the very depths of your soul and spirit. So be it,

ASSERTION # 24

We are now calling on the infinite power and eternal help of God, Jesus Christ, the Holy Ghost, and with absolute faith, gratitude, unconditional love for them and they for you, and with their great healing powers, and your sincere, heartfelt supplications, and their approval, and upon your prayerful request, they will now help you embrace and perfect the righteous element of humility. With determination and irreversible willpower, you will now positively act on this decision from this moment on and forever. You will now definitely honor this assertion, which will penetrate to the very depths of your soul and spirit. So be it.

ASSERTION # 25

We are now calling on the infinite power and eternal help of God, Jesus Christ, the Holy Ghost, and with absolute faith, gratitude, unconditional love for them and they for you, and with their great healing powers, and your sincere, heartfelt supplications, and their approval, and upon your prayerful request, they will now help you embrace and perfect the righteous element of humor. With determination and irreversible willpower, you will now positively act on this decision from this moment on and forever. You will now definitely honor this assertion, which will penetrate to the very depths of your soul and spirit. So be it.

ASSERTION # 26

We are now calling on the infinite power and eternal help of God, Jesus Christ, the Holy Ghost, and with absolute faith, gratitude, unconditional love for them and they for you, and with their great healing powers, and your sincere, heartfelt supplications, and their approval, and upon your prayerful request, they will now help you embrace and perfect the righteous element of industry. With determination and irreversible willpower, you will now positively act on this decision from this moment on and forever. You will now definitely honor this assertion, which will penetrate to the very depths of your soul and spirit. So be it.

ASSERTION # 27

We are now calling on the infinite power and eternal help of God, Jesus Christ the Holy Ghost, and with absolute faith, gratitude, unconditional love for them and they for you, and with their great healing powers, and your sincere, heartfelt supplications, and their approval, and upon your prayerful request, they will now help you embrace and perfect the righteous element of your inner light. With determination and irreversible willpower, you will now positively act on this decision from this moment on and forever. You will now definitely honor this assertion, which will penetrate to the very depths of your soul and spirit. So be it.

ASSERTION # 28

We are now calling on the infinite power and eternal help of God, Jesus Christ, the Holy Ghost, and with absolute faith, gratitude, unconditional love for them and they for you, and with their great healing powers, and your sincere, heartfelt supplications, and their approval, and upon your prayerful request, they will now help you embrace and perfect the righteous element of intelligence. With determination and irreversible willpower, you will now positively act on this decision from this moment on and forever. You will now definitely honor this assertion, which will penetrate to the very depths of your soul and spirit. So be it.

ASSERTION # 29

We are now calling on the infinite power and eternal help of God, Jesus Christ, the Holy Ghost, and with absolute faith, gratitude, unconditional love for them and they for you, and with their great healing powers, and your sincere, heartfelt supplications, and their approval, and upon your prayerful request, they will now help you embrace and perfect the righteous element of inquisitiveness. With determination and irreversible willpower, you will now positively act on this decision from this moment and forever. You will now definitely honor this assertion, which will penetrate to the very depths of your soul and spirit. So be it.

ASSERTION # 30

We are now calling on the infinite power and eternal help of God, Jesus Christ, the Holy Ghost, and with absolute faith, gratitude, unconditional love for them and they for you, and with their great healing powers, and your sincere, heartfelt supplications, and their approval, and upon your prayerful request, they will now help you embrace and perfect the righteous element of integrity. With determination and irreversible willpower, you will now positively act on this decision from this moment on and forever. You will now definitely honor this assertion, which will penetrate to the very depths of your soul and spirit. So be it.

ASSERTION # 31

We are now calling on the infinite power and eternal help of God, Jesus Christ, the Holy Ghost, and with absolute faith, gratitude, unconditional love for them and they for you, and with their great healing powers, and your sincere, heartfelt supplications, and their approval, and upon your prayerful request, they will now help you embrace and perfect the righteous element of intensions. With determination and irreversible willpower, you will now positively act on this decision from this moment on and forever. You will now definitely honor this assertion, which will penetrate to the very depths of your soul and spirit. So be it.

ASSERTION # 32

We are now calling on the infinite power and eternal help of God, Jesus Christ, the holy Ghost, and with absolute faith, gratitude, unconditional love for them and they for you, and with their great healing powers, and your sincere, heartfelt supplications, and their approval, and upon your prayerful request, they will now help you embrace and perfect the righteous element of justice. With determination and irreversible willpower, you will positively act on this decision from this moment on and forever. You will now definitely honor this assertion, which will penetrate to the very depths of your soul and spirit. So be it.

ASSERTION # 33

We are now calling on the infinite power and eternal help of God, Jesus Christ, the Holy Ghost, and with absolute faith, gratitude, unconditional love for them and they for you, and with their great healing powers, and your sincere, heartfelt supplications, and their approval, and upon your prayerful request, they will now help you embrace and perfect the righteous element of kindness. With determination and irreversible willpower, you will positively act on this decision from this moment on and forever. You will now definitely honor this assertion, which will penetrate to the very depths of your soul and spirit. So be it.

ASSERTION # 34

We are now calling on the infinite power and eternal help of God, Jesus Christ, the Holy Ghost, and with absolute faith, gratitude, unconditional love for them and they for you, and with their great healing powers, and your sincere, heartfelt supplications, and their approval, and upon your prayerful request, they will now help you embrace and perfect the righteous element of knowledge. With determination and irreversible willpower, you will positively act on this decision from this moment on and forever. You will now definitely honor this assertion, which will penetrate to the very depths of your soul and spirit. So be it.

ASSERTION # 35

We are now calling on the infinite power and eternal help of God, Jesus Christ, the Holy Ghost, and with absolute faith, gratitude, unconditional love for them and they for you, and with their great healing powers, and your sincere, heartfelt supplications, and their approval, and upon your prayerful request, they will now help you embrace and perfect the righteous element of love. With determination and irreversible willpower, you will positively act on this decision from this moment on and forever. You will now definitely honor this assertion, which will penetrate to the very depths of your soul and spirit. So be it.

ASSERTION # 36

We are now calling on the infinite power and eternal help of God, Jesus Christ, the Holy Ghost, and with absolute faith, gratitude, unconditional love for them and they for you, and with their great healing powers, and your sincere, heartfelt supplications, and their approval, They will now help you embrace and perfect the righteous element of loyalty. With determination and irreversible willpower, you will positively act on this decision from this moment on and forever. You will now definitely honor this assertion, which will penetrate to the very depths of your soul and spirit. So be it.

ASSERTION # 37

We are now calling on the infinite power and eternal help of God, Jesus Christ, the Holy Ghost, and with absolute faith, gratitude, unconditional love for them and they for you, with their great healing powers, and with your sincere, heartfelt supplications, and with their approval, and upon your prayerful request, they will now help you embrace and perfect the righteous element of meekness. With determination and irreversible willpower, you will positively act on this decision from this moment on and forever. You will now definitely honor this assertion, which will penetrate to the very depths of your soul and spirit. So be it.

ASSERTION # 38

We are now calling on the infinite power and eternal help of God, Jesus Christ, the Holy Ghost, and with absolute faith, gratitude, unconditional love for them and they for you, and with their great healing powers, and your sincere, heartfelt supplications, and their approval, and upon your prayerful request, they will now help you embrace and perfect the righteous element of mercy. With determination and irreversible willpower, you will positively act on this decision from this moment on and forever. You will now definitely honor this assertion, which will penetrate to the very depths of your soul and spirit. So be it.

ASSERTION # 39

We are now calling on the infinite power and eternal help of God, Jesus Christ, the Holy Ghost, and with absolute faith, gratitude, unconditional love for them and they for you, and with their great healing powers, and your sincere, heartfelt supplications, and their approval, and upon your prayerful request, they will now help you embrace and perfect the righteous element of meditation. With determination and irreversible willpower, you will positively act on this decision from this moment on and forever. You will now definitely honor this assertion, which will penetrate to the very depths of your soul and spirit. So be it.

ASSERTION # 40

We are now calling on the infinite power and eternal help of God, Jesus Christ, the Holy Ghost, and with absolute faith, gratitude, unconditional love for them and they for you, and with their great healing powers, and your sincere, heartfelt supplications and their approval, and upon your prayerful request, they will now help you embrace and perfect the righteous element of modesty. With determination and irreversible willpower, you will positively act on this decision from this moment on and forever. You will now definitely honor this assertion, which will penetrate to the very depths of your soul and spirit. So be it.

ASSERTION # 41

We are now calling on the infinite power and eternal help of God, Jesus Christ, the Holy Ghost, and with absolute faith, gratitude, unconditional love for them and they for you, and with their great healing powers, and your sincere, heartfelt supplications, and their approval, and upon your prayerful request, they will now help you embrace and perfect the righteous element of morality. With determination and irreversible willpower, you will positively act on this decision from this moment on and forever. You will now definitely honor this assertion, which will penetrate to the very soul and spirit. So be it.

ASSERTION # 42

We are now calling on the infinite power and eternal help of God, Jesus Christ, the Holy Ghost, and with absolute faith, gratitude, unconditional love for them and they for you, and with their great healing powers, and your sincere, heartfelt supplications, and their approval, and upon your prayerful request, they will now help you embrace and perfect the righteous element of motivation. With determination and irreversible willpower, you will positively act on this decision from this moment on and forever. So be it.

ASSERTION # 43

We are now calling on the infinite power and eternal help of God, Jesus Christ, the Holy Ghost, and with absolute faith, gratitude, unconditional love for them and they for you, and with their great healing powers, and your sincere, heartfelt supplications, and their approval, and upon your prayerful request, they will now help you embrace and perfect the righteous element of obedience. With determination and irreversible willpower, you will positively act on this decision from this moment on and forever. So be it.

ASSERTION # 44

We are now calling on the infinite power and eternal help of God, Jesus Christ, the Holy Ghost, and with absolute faith, gratitude, unconditional love for them and they for you, and with their great healing powers, and your sincere, heartfelt supplications, and their approval, and upon your prayerful request, they will now help you embrace and perfect the righteous element of organization. With determination and irreversible willpower, you will positively act on this decision from this moment on and forever. So be it.

ASSERTION # 45

We are now calling on the infinite power and eternal help of God, Jesus Christ, the Holy Ghost, and with absolute faith, gratitude, unconditional love for them and they for you, and with their great healing powers, and your sincere, heartfelt supplications, and their approval, and upon your prayerful request, they will now help you embrace and perfect the righteous element of patience. With determination and irreversible willpower, you will now positively act on this decision from this moment on and forever. So be it.

ASSERTION # 46

We are now calling on the infinite power and eternal help of God, Jesus Christ, the Holy Ghost, and with absolute faith, gratitude, unconditional love for them and they for you, and with their great healing powers, and your sincere, heartfelt supplications, and their approval, and upon your prayerful request, they will now help you embrace and perfect the righteous element of persistence. With determination and irreversible willpower, you will now positively act on this decision from this moment on and forever. So be it.

ASSERTION # 47

We are now calling on the infinite power and eternal help of God, Jesus Christ, the Holy Ghost, and with absolute faith, gratitude, unconditional love for them and they for you, and with their great healing powers, and your sincere, heartfelt supplications, and their approval, and upon your prayerful request, they will now help you embrace and perfect the righteous element of preparedness. With determination and irreversible willpower, you will now positively act on this decision from this moment on and forever. So be it.

ASSERTION # 48

We are now calling on the infinite power and eternal help of God, Jesus Christ, the Holy Ghost, and with absolute faith, gratitude, unconditional love for them and they for you, and with their great healing powers, and your sincere, heartfelt supplications, and their approval, and upon your prayerful request, they will now help you embrace and perfect the righteous element of promptness. With determination and irreversible willpower, you will now positively act on this decision from this moment on and forever. So be it.

ASSERTION # 49

We are now calling on the infinite power and eternal help of God, Jesus Christ, the Holy Ghost, and with absolute faith, gratitude, unconditional love for them and they for you, and with their great healing powers, and your sincere, heartfelt supplications, and their approval, and upon your prayerful request, they will now help you embrace and perfect the righteous element of purity. With determination and irreversible willpower, you will now positively act on this decision from this moment on and forever. So be it.

ASSERTION # 50

We are now calling on the infinite power and eternal help of God, Jesus Christ, the Holy Ghost, and with absolute faith, gratitude, unconditional love for them and they for you, and with their great healing powers, and your sincere, heartfelt supplications, and their approval, and upon your prayerful request, they will now help you embrace and perfect the righteous element of repentance. With determination and irreversible willpower, you will now act on this decision from this moment on and forever. So be it.

ASSERTION # 51

We are now calling on the infinite power and eternal help of God, Jesus Christ, the Holy Ghost, and with absolute faith, gratitude, unconditional love for them and they for you, and with their great healing powers, and your sincere, heartfelt supplications, and their approval, and upon your prayerful request, they will now help you embrace and perfect the righteous element of resilience. With determination and irreversible willpower, you will now act on this decision from this moment on and forever. So be it.

ASSERTION # 52

We are now calling on the infinite power and eternal help of God, Jesus Christ, the Holy Ghost, and with absolute faith, gratitude, unconditional love for them and they for you, and with their great healing powers, and your sincere, heartfelt supplications, and their approval, and upon your prayerful request, they will now help you embrace and perfect the righteous element of being resolute. With determination and irreversible willpower, you will now act on this decision from this moment on and forever. So be it.

ASSERTION # 53

We are now calling on the infinite power and eternal help of God, Jesus Christ, the Holy Ghost, and with absolute faith, gratitude, unconditional love for them and they for you, and with their great healing powers, and your sincere, heartfelt supplications, and their approval, and upon your prayerful request, they will now help you embrace and perfect the righteous element of responsibility. With determination and irreversible willpower, you will now act on this decision from this moment on and forever. So be it.

ASSERTION # 54

We are now calling on the infinite power and eternal help of God, Jesus Christ, the Holy Ghost, and with absolute faith, gratitude, unconditional love for them and they for you, and with their great healing powers, and your sincere, heartfelt supplications, and their approval, and upon your prayerful request, they will now help you embrace and perfect the righteous element of reverence. With determination and irreversible willpower, you will now act on this decision from this moment on and forever. So be it.

ASSERTION # 55

We are now calling on the infinite power and eternal help of God, Jesus Christ, the Holy Ghost, and with absolute faith, gratitude, unconditional love for them and they for you, and with their great healing powers, and your sincere, heartfelt supplications, and with their approval, and upon your prayerful request, they will now help you embrace and perfect the righteous element of righteousness. With determination and irreversible willpower, you will now act on this decision from this moment on and forever. So be it.

ASSERTION # 56

We are now calling on the infinite power and eternal help of God, Jesus Christ, the Holy Ghost, and with absolute faith, gratitude, unconditional love for them and they for you, and with their great healing powers, and your sincere, heartfelt supplications, and their approval, and upon your prayerful request, they will now help you embrace and perfect the righteous element of sacrifice. With determination and irreversible willpower, you will now act on this decision from this moment on and forever. So be it.

ASSERTION # 57

We are now calling on the infinite power and eternal help of God, Jesus Christ, the Holy Ghost, and with absolute faith, gratitude, unconditional love for them and they for you, and with their great healing powers, and your sincere, heartfelt supplications, and their approval, and upon your prayerful request, they will now help you embrace and perfect the righteous element of self-discipline. With determination and irreversible willpower, you will now act on this decision from this moment on and forever. So be it.

ASSERTION # 58

We are now calling on the infinite power and eternal help of God, Jesus Christ, the Holy Ghost, and with absolute faith, gratitude, unconditional love for them and they for you, and with their great healing powers, and your sincere, heartfelt supplications, and their approval, and upon your prayerful request, they will now help you embrace and perfect the righteous element of self-esteem. With determination and irreversible willpower, you will now act on this decision from this moment on and forever. So be it.

ASSERTION # 59

We are now calling on the infinite power and eternal help of God, Jesus Christ, the Holy Ghost, and with absolute faith, gratitude, unconditional love for them and they for you, and with their great healing powers, and your sincere, heartfelt supplications, and their approval, and upon your prayerful request, they will now help you embrace and perfect the righteous element of self-reliance. With determination and irreversible willpower, you will now act on this decision from this moment on and forever. So be it.

ASSERTION # 60

We are now calling on the infinite power and eternal help of God, Jesus Christ, the Holy Ghost, and with absolute faith, gratitude, unconditional love for them and they for you, and with their great healing powers, and your sincere, heartfelt supplications, and their approval, and upon your prayerful request they will now help you embrace and perfect the righteous element of sensitivity. With determination and irreversible willpower, you will now act on this decision from this moment on and forever. So be it.

ASSERTION # 61

We are now calling on the infinite power and eternal help of God, Jesus Christ, the Holy Ghost, and with absolute faith, gratitude, unconditional love for them and they for you, and with their great healing powers, and your sincere, heartfelt supplications, and their approval, and upon prayerful request, they will now help you embrace and perfect the righteous element of serenity. With determination and irreversible will power, you will now act on this decision from this moment on and forever. So be it.

ASSERTION # 62

We are now calling on the infinite power and eternal help of God, Jesus Christ, the Holy Ghost, and with absolute faith, gratitude, unconditional love for them and they for you, and with their great healing powers, and your sincere, heartfelt supplications, and their approval, and upon your prayerful request, they will now help you embrace and perfect the righteous element of sharing. With determination and irreversible will power, you will now act on this decision from this moment on and forever. So be it.

ASSERTION # 63

We re now calling on the infinite power and eternal help of God, Jesus Christ, the Holy Ghost, and with absolute faith, gratitude, unconditional love for them and they for you, and with their great healing powers, and your sincere, heartfelt supplications, and their approval, and upon your prayerful request, they will now help you embrace and perfect the righteous element of spirituality. With determination and irreversible willpower, you will now act on this decision from this moment on and forever. So be it.

ASSERTION # 64

We are now calling on the infinite power and eternal help of God, Jesus Christ, the Holy Ghost, and with absolute faith, gratitude, unconditional love for them and they for you, and with their great healing powers, and your sincere, heartfelt supplications, and their approval, and upon your prayerful request, they will now help you embrace and perfect the righteous element of stability. With determination and irreversible willpower, you will now act on this decision from this moment on and forever. So be it.

ASSERTION # 65

We are now calling on the infinite power and eternal help of God, Jesus Christ, the Holy Ghost, and with absolute faith, gratitude, unconditional love for them and they for you, and with their great healing powers, and your sincere, heartfelt supplications, and their approval, and upon your prayerful request, they will now help you embrace and perfect the righteous element of being steadfast. With determination and irreversible willpower, you will now act on this decision from this moment on and forever. So be it.

ASSERTION # 66

We are now calling on the infinite power and eternal help of God, Jesus Christ, the Holy Ghost, and with absolute faith, gratitude, unconditional love for them and they for you, and with their great healing powers, and your sincere, heartfelt supplications, and their approval, and upon your prayerful request, they will now help you embrace and perfect the righteous element of strength. With determination and irreversible willpower, you will now act on this decision from this moment on and forever. You will now definitely honor this assertion, which will penetrate to the very depths of your soul and spirit. So be it.

ASSERTION # 67

We are now calling on the infinite power and eternal help of God, Jesus Christ, the Holy Ghost, and with absolute faith, gratitude, unconditional love for them and they for you, and with their great healing powers, and your sincere, heartfelt supplications, and their approval, and upon your prayerful request, they will now help you embrace and perfect the righteous element of being studious. With determination and irreversible willpower, you will now act on this decision from this moment on and forever. You will now definitely honor this assertion, which will penetrate to the very depths of your soul and spirit. So be it.

ASSERTION # 68

We are now calling on the infinite power and eternal help of God, Jesus Christ, the Holy Ghost, and with absolute faith, gratitude, unconditional love for them and they for you, and with their great healing powers, and your sincere, heartfelt supplications, and their approval, and upon your prayerful request, they will now help you embrace and perfect the righteous element of being success oriented. With determination and irreversible willpower, you will now act on this decision from this moment on and forever. You will definitely honor this assertion, which will penetrate to the very depths of your soul and spirit. So be it.

ASSERTION # 69

We are now calling on the infinite power and eternal help of God, Jesus Christ, the Holy Ghost, and with absolute faith, gratitude, unconditional love for them and they for you, and with their great healing powers, and with your sincere, heartfelt supplications, and with their approval, and upon your prayerful request, they will now help you embrace and perfect the righteous element of surrendering. With determination and irreversible willpower, you will now act on this decision from this moment on and forever. You will definitely honor this assertion, which will penetrate to the very depths of your soul and spirit. So be it.

ASSERTION # 70

We are now calling on the infinite power and eternal help of God, Jesus Christ, the Holy Ghost, and with absolute faith, gratitude, unconditional love for them and they for you, and with their great healing powers, and your sincere, heartfelt supplications, and their approval, and upon your prayerful request, they will now help you embrace and perfect the righteous element of being tactful. With determination and irreversible willpower, you will now act on this decision from this moment on and forever. You will definitely honor this assertion, which will penetrate to the very depths of your soul and spirit. So be it.

ASSERTION # 71

We are now calling on the infinite power and eternal help of God, Jesus Christ, the Holy Ghost, and with absolute faith, gratitude, unconditional love for them and they for you, and with their great healing powers, and your sincere, heartfelt supplications, and their approval, and upon your prayerful request, they will now help you embrace and perfect the righteous element of being temperate. With determination and irreversible willpower, you will now act on this decision from this moment on and forever. You will definitely honor this assertion, which will penetrate to the very depths of your soul and spirit. So be it.

ASSERTION # 72

We are now calling on the infinite power and eternal help of God, Jesus Christ, the Holy Ghost, and with absolute faith, gratitude, unconditional love for them and they for you, and with their great healing powers, and your sincere, heartfelt supplications, and their approval, and upon your prayerful request, they will now help you embrace and perfect the righteous element of being thoughtful. With determination and irreversible willpower, you will now act on this decision from this moment on and forever. You will definitely honor this assertion, which will penetrate to the very depths of your soul and spirit.. So be it.

ASSERTION # 73

We are now calling on the infinite power and eternal help of God, Jesus Christ, the Holy Ghost, and with absolute faith, gratitude, unconditional love for them and they for you, and with their great healing powers, and your sincere, heartfelt supplications, and their approval, and upon your prayerful request, they will now help you embrace and perfect the righteous element of being trustworthy. With determination and irreversible willpower, you will now act on this decision from this moment on and forever. You will definitely honor this assertion, which will penetrate to the very depths of your soul and spirit. So be it.

ASSERTION # 74

We are now calling on the infinite power and eternal help of God, Jesus Christ, the Holy Ghost, and with absolute faith, gratitude, unconditional love for them and they for you, and with their great healing powers, and your sincere, heartfelt supplications, and their approval They will now help you embrace and perfect the righteous element of truthfulness. With determination and irreversible willpower, you will now act on this decision from this moment on and forever. You will definitely honor this assertion, which will penetrate to the very depths of your soul and spirit. So be it.

ASSERTION # 75

We are now calling on the infinite power and eternal help of God, Jesus Christ, the Holy Ghost, and with absolute faith, gratitude, unconditional love for them and they for you, and with their great healing powers, and your sincere, heartfelt supplications, and their approval, and upon your prayerful request, they will now help you embrace and perfect the righteous element of being virtuous. With determination and irreversible willpower, you will now act on this decision from this moment on and forever. You will definitely honor this assertion, which will penetrate to the very depths of your soul and spirit. So be it.

ASSERTION # 76

We are now calling on the infinite power and eternal help of God, Jesus Christ, the Holy Ghost, and with absolute faith, gratitude, unconditional love for them and they for you, and with their great healing powers, and your sincere, heartfelt supplications, and their approval, and upon your prayerful request they will now help you embrace and perfect the righteous element of being forever watchful. With determination and irreversible willpower, you will now act on this decision from this moment on and forever. You will definitely honor this assertion, which will penetrate to the very depths of your soul and spirit. So be it.

ASSERTION # 77

We are now calling on the infinite power and eternal help of God, Jesus Christ, the Holy Ghost, and with absolute faith, gratitude, unconditional love for them and they for you, and with their great healing powers, and your sincere, heartfelt supplications, and their approval, and upon your prayerful request, they will now help you embrace and perfect the righteous element of wisdom. With determination and irreversible willpower, you will now act on this decision from this moment on and forever. You will definitely honor this assertion, which will penetrate to the very depths of your soul and spirit. So be it.

Chapter Seven

ANOTHER FORMAT

WITH OUR BUSY SCHEDULES IT is necessary that time be set aside, about ten to fifteen minutes, each morning and evening for these affirmations. Select a time when you can be alone with no outside interferences. Repeat each affirmation, boldly, loudly with conviction and authority. To repeat them in an even monotone, or even a normal voice with no emotion and without any conviction, will not be effective.

Listed below are affirmations that have worked well for me, Affirmations are a form of self-hypnosis or self-induction, although you won't be in a state of trance for them to be effective.

Always be loud, decisive, convincing, and very determined to get the best results. If you are not convincing to yourself, your desired outcome will be less effective. Be positive; be sure.

The outcome you desire will depend on consistency, determination, follow-thru and commitment. If you're not convincing to yourself and committed don't even start.

To be effective you should only select no more than two affirmations per session. More than that may have an adverse effect on the outcome you desire. Repeat each selected affirmation at least four or five times, twice daily, for a period of, at least, one month, to have the maximum effect, before selecting another set of affirmations. You may feel you need more than four or five repetitions. Do as many as will accomplish your goal.

The affirmations presented here include many conditions, situations, and if needed could be tailored to your own personal needs. For the greatest effect, God, Christ and the Holy Ghost should always be included in any affirmation that you personally create.

These affirmations are in no specific order; I wrote them as they came to me. Each one you select should help you overcome, conquer, and rise above some of the afflictions that hinder your spiritual growth and health.

You will continue to be the creator of many of your afflictions until you decide that you are no longer satisfied with who and what you are and make the necessary changes to become what and who you hope to become through assertions and affirmations.

AFFIRMATION # 1

Having disease, illness, or dysfunction is no longer a statement of what and who I am or want to become and I acknowledge that I am the major contributor, on a conscious and subconscious level, of many of my illnesses, diseases and dysfunctions. The purpose for which they were created no longer exists, and they are no longer needed or wanted. So with the infinite power and help of God, Jesus Christ, the Holy Ghost, and with absolute faith, conviction, gratitude, unconditional love for them and they for me I now choose the total rejection of all fears, sympathies, beliefs, attitudes, expressions, behaviors or wants that has drawn to me any illness, disease or dysfunction. I will definitely act on this crucial decision from this moment on and forever. I will definitely honor this affirmation, which will penetrate to the very depths of my soul and spirit. So be it.

AFFIRMATION # 2

With the infinite power and help of God, Jesus Christ, the Holy Ghost, and with absolute faith, conviction, gratitude, unconditional love for them and they for me, I now choose to trust God, Jesus Christ and the Holy Ghost, implicitly, and I will accept their love more freely and thankfully. I will magnify their love, expand it in my life, and extend it to all with whom I come in contact. I will definitely act on this crucial decision from this moment on and forever. I will absolutely honor this affirmation, which will penetrate to the very depths of my soul and spirit So be it.

AFFIRMATION # 3

With the infinite power and help of God, Jesus Christ, the Holy Ghost, and with absolute faith, conviction, gratitude, unconditional love for them and they for me, I now choose to trust myself, with the help of God, in every decision I make. Self-trust is extremely important in my life. With Gods help I will create and nurture it until it is a very vital part of my life. I will definitely act on this crucial decision from this moment on and forever. I will definitely honor this affirmation, which will penetrate to the very depths of my soul and spirit. So be it.

AFFIRMATION # 4

With the infinite power and help of God, Jesus Christ, the Holy Ghost, and with absolute faith, conviction, gratitude, unconditional love for them and they for me I now choose to rid myself of all destructive emotions i.e.,, pain, shame, anger, guilt, hate, resentment and frustration, associated with my life in an adverse way. I will definitely act on this crucial decision from this moment on and forever. I will definitely honor this affirmation, which will penetrate to the very depths of my soul and spirit. So be it.

AFFIRMATION # 5

With the infinite power and help of God, Jesus Christ, the Holy Ghost, and with absolute faith, conviction, gratitude, unconditional love for and from them I now choose to create the extraordinary experience of increasing my great love for God, Jesus Christ, and the Holy Ghost daily. I will always express it to all with whom I come in contact. With complete determination and irreversible willpower, I will definitely act on this crucial decision from this moment on and forever. I will definitely honor this affirmation, which will penetrate to the very depths of my soul and spirit. So be it.

AFFIRMATION # 6

With the infinite power and help of God, Jesus Christ, the Holy Ghost, and with absolute faith, conviction, gratitude, unconditional love for and from them I now choose to increase my faith each and every day with affirmations to increase my health, vitality and bring to fruition to all of my righteous goals. With complete determination and irreversible willpower, I will definitely act on this crucial decision from this moment on and forever. I will definitely honor this affirmation, which will penetrate to the very depths of my soul and spirit. So be it.

AFFIRMATION # 7

With the infinite power and help of God, Jesus Christ, the Holy Ghost, and with absolute faith, conviction, gratitude, unconditional love for and from them I now choose to overcome all doubts, and un-beliefs concerning the implementation of every affirmation I select. Each affirmation will increases my righteousness, health, spiritual growth and general well being. With complete determination and irreversible willpower I will definitely act on this crucial decision from this moment on and forever. I will absolutely honor this affirmation, which will penetrate to the very depths of my soul and spirit. So be it.

AFFIRMATION # 8

With the infinite power and help of God, Jesus Christ, the Holy Ghost, and with absolute faith, conviction, gratitude, unconditional love for and from them I now choose to know that I deserve to implement every affirmation I select to increase my righteousness, health, talents, abilities, spiritual growth, general well being and God's blessings. With compete determination and irreversible willpower I will definitely act on this crucial decision from this moment on and forever. I will absolutely honor this affirmation, which will penetrate to the very depths of my soul and spirit. So be it.

AFFIRMATION # 9

With the infinite power and help of God, Jesus Christ, the Holy Ghost, and with absolute faith, conviction, Gratitude, unconditional love for and from them. I now choose to forgive myself for all past indiscretions and all emotional trauma, which has resulted from past events. With complete determination and irreversible willpower I will definitely act on this crucial decision from this moment on and forever. I will absolutely honor this affirmation, which will penetrate to the very depths of my soul and spirit. So be it.

AFFIRMATION # 10

With the infinite power and help of God, Jesus Christ, the Holy Ghost, and with absolute faith, conviction, gratitude, unconditional love for and from them, I now choose to create the wonderful experience of enjoying abundance, prosperity and happiness in every aspect of my life. With complete determination and irreversible willpower I will definitely act on this crucial decision from this moment on and forever. I will absolutely honor this affirmation, which will penetrate to the very depth of my soul and spirit. So be it.

AFFIRMATION # 11

With the infinite power and help of God, Jesus Christ, the Holy Ghost, and with absolute faith, conviction, gratitude, and unconditional love for and from them, I now choose to overcome my inability to fall asleep and remain asleep for the entire night. Should nature call during the night I will be able to fall asleep again after the call, and remain asleep for the remainder of the night. With complete determination and irreversible willpower I will definitely act on this crucial decision from this moment on and forever. I will absolutely honor this affirmation, which will penetrate to the very depths of my soul and spirit. So be it.

AFFIRMATION # 12

With the infinite power and help of God, Jesus Christ, the Holy Ghost, and with absolute faith conviction, gratitude, unconditional love for and from them I now choose to seek the Lord's help through prayer, scripture study, obedience, charity and listening to the still small voice to always direct my life. With complete determination and irreversible willpower I will now definitely act on this crucial decision from this moment on and forever. I will absolutely honor this affirmation, which will penetrate to the very depths of my soul and spirit. So be it.

AFFIRMATION # 13

With the infinite power and help of God, Jesus Christ, the Holy Ghost, and with absolute faith, conviction, gratitude, unconditional love for and from them I now choose to identify, overcome, conquer, and rise above all challenges, obstacles, afflictions, problems, and adversities, with the help of God. With complete determination and irreversible willpower I will definitely act of this crucial decision from this moment on and forever. I will absolutely honor this affirmation, which will penetrate to the very depths of my soul and spirit. So be it.

AFFIRMATION # 14

With the infinite power and help of God, Jesus Christ, the Holy Ghost, and with absolute faith, conviction, gratitude, unconditional love for and from them, I now choose to select spiritual growth and refrain from unrighteousness and ungodliness. With complete determination and irreversible willpower I will definitely act on this crucial decision from this moment on and forever. I will absolutely honor this affirmation, which will penetrate to the very depths of my soul and spirit. So be it.

AFFIRMATION # 15

Having disease, illness or dysfunction is no longer a true statement of who and what I am or want to become and I acknowledge that I am the sole creator (on a conscious and subconscious level), of many of my illnesses and dysfunctions. The purpose for which they were created no longer exists, and is no longer wanted or needed because I have repented, and have been forgiven of them. So with the infinite power and help from God, Jesus Christ and the Holy Ghost, and with absolute faith, conviction, gratitude, unconditional love for and from Them, I now choose to create for me, with absolute power a total rejection of all guilt, fear, sympathy, beliefs, attitudes, expressions, behavior, and shame that has drawn to me any illness, disease, or dysfunction in the past or present. With complete faith, determination and irreversible willpower I will now definitely act on this crucial decision from this moment on and forever. I will convincingly honor this affirmation, which will penetrate to the very depths of my soul and spirit. So be it.

AFFIRMATION # 16

With the infinite power and help of God, Jesus Christ and the Holy Ghost, and with unwavering faith, conviction, gratitude, unconditional love for and from them I now choose to create a complete cessation of all thinking and behavior that produces any unrighteous emotional pain, fear, hate, shame, anger, guilt, resentment, illness, and un-forgiveness. With determination and irreversible willpower I will now definitely act on this crucial decision from this moment on and forever. I will absolutely honor this affirmation, which will penetrate to the very depths of my soul and spirit. So be it.

AFFIRMATION # 17

With the infinite power and help of God, Jesus Christ, the Holy Ghost, and with unwavering faith, conviction, gratitude, unconditional love for and from them I now choose to forgive myself for all of the things I have said or done that has brought distress or pain to me or anyone else. With complete faith, determination and irreversible willpower I will now definitely act on this crucial decision from this moment on and forever. I will absolutely honor this affirmation, which will penetrate to the very depths of my soul and spirit. So be it.

AFFIRMATION # 18

With the infinite power and help of God, Jesus Christ, the Holy Ghost, and with absolute faith, conviction, gratitude, unconditional love for and from them I now choose to release and reject those destructive fears that have produced any illnesses, diseases or impairments of my mind and body. With complete determination and irreversible willpower I will now definitely act on this crucial decision from this moment on and forever. I will absolutely honor this affirmation, which will penetrate to the very depths of my soul and spirit. So be it.

AFFIRMATION # 19

With the infinite power and help of God, Jesus Christ, the Holy Ghost, and with absolute conviction, gratitude, unwavering faith, unconditional love for and from them I now choose to be completely free of illness, disease and impairment of my mind and body. With complete faith, determination and irreversible willpower I will now definitely act on this crucial decision from this moment on and forever. I will absolutely honor this affirmation, which will penetrate to the very depths of my soul and spirit. So be it.

AFFIRMATION # 20

With the infinite power and help of God, Jesus Christ, the Holy Ghost, and with absolute conviction, gratitude, unwavering faith, unconditional love for and from them I now choose to be forgiving of any experience, in my life that has produced hate, fear, anger, guilt, shame, hostility, frustration, worry, un-forgiveness, resentment and feelings of betrayal that has produced within me any mental pain or illness. With complete faith, determination and irreversible willpower I will now definitely act on this crucial decision from this moment on and forever. I will absolutely honor this affirmation, which will penetrate to the very depths of my soul and spirit. So be it.

AFFIRMATION # 21

With the infinite power and help of God, Jesus Christ, the Holy Ghost, and with absolute conviction, gratitude, unwavering faith, unconditional love for and from them I now choose to be completely free of any desire or need that generates within me any illness, pain or Dysfunction, which attracts sympathy, attention, or pity from others. These wants or desires no longer define what or who I am, so they no longer exist. With complete faith, determination and irreversible willpower I will now definitely act on this crucial decision now and forever. I will definitely honor this affirmation, which will penetrate to the very depths of my soul and spirit. So be it.

AFFIRMATION # 22

With the infinite power and help of God, Jesus Christ, the Holy Ghost, and with absolute conviction, gratitude, unwavering faith, unconditional love for and from them, I now choose to be totally and completely forgiving of myself for all actions that has brought any physical, mental or emotional pain or stress to me or others. With complete faith, determination and irreversible willpower I will now definitely act on this crucial decision from this moment on and forever. I will absolutely honor this affirmation, which will penetrate to the very depths of my soul and spirit. So be it.

AFFIRMATION # 23

With the infinite power and help of God, Jesus Christ, the Holy Ghost, and with absolute conviction, gratitude, unwavering faith, unconditional love for and from them, I now choose to be completely accepting of Gods forgiveness, allowing him to fill my mind and body with love so that I may express it to myself and all with whom I come in contact, with happiness and joy through service, compassion, kindness, acceptance, honesty, integrity and morality. With complete faith, determination and irreversible willpower I will now definitely act on this crucial decision from this moment on and forever. I will definitely honor this affirmation, which will penetrate to the very depths of my soul and spirit. So be it.

AFFIRMATION # 24

With the infinite power and help from God, Jesus Christ, the Holy Ghost, and with absolute conviction, gratitude, faith, unconditional love for and from them, I now choose to increase my love for myself with each passing day and to express it to all others with whom I come in contact. With absolute faith, determination and irreversible willpower, I will now definitely act on this crucial decision from this moment on and forever. I will definitely honor this affirmation, which will penetrate to the very depth of my soul and spirit. So be it.

AFFIRMATION # 25

With the infinite power and help from God, Jesus Christ, The Holy Ghost, and with absolute conviction, gratitude, faith, unconditional love for and from them, I now choose to balance my endocrine system with each gland producing the exact amount of glandular fluid necessary to maintain and enhance my life with health and vitality. With absolute faith, determination and irreversible willpower, I will now definitely act on this crucial decision from this moment on and forever. I will absolutely honor this affirmation, which will penetrate to the very depths of my soul and spirit. So be it.

AFFIRMATION #26

With the infinite power and help from God, Jesus Christ, the holy Ghost, and with absolute conviction, gratitude, unwavering faith, unconditional love for and from them, I now choose to be one with God and know myself as the magnificent and marvelous being created by Him. With unwavering faith, determination and irreversible willpower, I will now definitely act on this crucial decision from this moment on and forever. I will absolutely honor this affirmation, which will penetrate to the very depths of my soul and spirit. So be it.

AFFIRMATION # 27

With the infinite power and help from God, Jesus Christ, the Holy Ghost, and with absolute conviction, gratitude, unwavering faith, unconditional love, for and from them, I now choose to completely cleanse my mind and body of all pollutants, which interfere with normal function. This cleansing will be an on-going process every day of my life. With absolute faith, determination and irreversible willpower, I will now certainly act on this crucial decision from this moment on and forever. I will definitely honor this affirmation, which will penetrate to the very depths of my soul and spirit. So be it.

AFFIRMATION # 28

With the infinite power and help from God, Jesus Christ, the Holy Ghost, and with absolute conviction, gratitude, unwavering faith, unconditional love for and from them, I now choose to continually attract the infinite healing powers of heaven to penetrate and permeate every cell of my mind and body, bathing them with the energies of love and life, producing a harmonious relationship between all cells. Every cell in my body and mind will become revitalized, healed and in harmony with all other cells. All of my physiological systems will function perfectly. With absolute faith, determination and irreversible willpower, I will now definitely act on this crucial decision from now on and forever. I will absolutely honor this affirmation, which will penetrate to the very depths of my soul and spirit. So be it.

AFFIRMATION # 29

With the infinite power and help from God, Jesus Christ, the Holy Ghost, and with absolute conviction, gratitude, unwavering faith, unconditional love for and from them, I now choose to forgive all who have wronged or injured me in any way. With absolute faith, determination and irreversible willpower, I will now positively act on this crucial decision from this moment on and forever. I will definitely honor this affirmation, which will penetrate to the very depths of my soul and spirit. So be it.

AFFIRMATION # 30

With the infinite power and help from God, Jesus Christ, the Holy Ghost, and with absolute conviction, gratitude, unwavering faith, unconditional love for and from them, I now choose to forgive myself of and release all my internal fear, anger, hate, prejudice, shame, doubt, hostility, guilt, resentment, frustration, and un-forgiveness. With absolute faith, determination and irreversible willpower, I will now definitely act on this crucial decision from this moment on and forever. I will positively honor this affirmation, which will penetrate to the very depths of my soul and spirit. So be it.

AFFIRMATION # 31

With the infinite power and help of God, Jesus Christ, The Holy Ghost, and with absolute conviction, gratitude, unwavering faith, unconditional love for and from them, I now choose to reject all destructive beliefs, attitudes, appetites, opinions, habits, desires, and compulsions that have caused me any illness, pain, discomfort, disease, or dysfunction within my mind and body. With absolute faith, determination and irreversible willpower, I will now definitely act on this crucial decision from this moment on and forever. I will positively honor this affirmation, which will penetrate to the very depths of my soul and spirit. So be it.

AFFIRMATION # 32

With the infinite power and help of God, Jesus Christ, The Holy Ghost, and with absolute conviction, gratitude, unwavering faith, unconditional love for and from them, I now choose to eliminate all beliefs, thinking and behavior that has brought me pain, hostility, fear, anger, guilt, shame, resentment, betrayal, doubt and un-forgiveness. With absolute faith, determination and irreversible willpower, I will now definitely, act on this crucial decision from now on and forever. I will positively honor this affirmation, which will penetrate to the very soul and spirit. So be it.

AFFIRMATION # 33

With the infinite power and help from God, Jesus Christ, the Holy Ghost, and with absolute conviction, gratitude, unwavering faith, and unconditional love for and from them, I now choose to enjoy abundance, prosperity and happiness in every aspect of my life. With unwavering faith, determination and absolute willpower I will now definitely act on this crucial decision from this moment on and forever. I will positively honor this affirmation, which will penetrate to the very depths of my soul and spirit. So be it.

AFFIRMATION # 34

With the infinite power and help of God, Jesus Christ, the Holy Ghost, and with absolute conviction, gratitude, unwavering faith, unconditional love for and from them I now choose to forgive and reject all thoughts, episodes and events in my life that has produced any fear which has caused me pain, illness, disease, dysfunction, un-forgiveness or unhappiness. With absolute faith, determination and irreversible willpower, I will now definitely act on this crucial decision from this moment on and forever. I will positively honor this affirmation, which will penetrate to the very depths of my soul and spirit. So be it.

AFFIRMATION # 35

With the infinite power and help of God, Jesus Christ, the Holy Ghost, and with absolute faith, conviction, gratitude, unconditional love for and from them I now choose to completely release all of my destructive beliefs, attitudes, appetites, opinions, prejudices, habits, compulsions and destructive desires. With absolute faith, determination and irreversible willpower, I will definitely act on this crucial decision from this moment on and forever. I will now positively honor this affirmation, which will penetrate to the very depths of my soul and spirit. So be it.

AFFIRMATION # 36

With the infinite power and help of God, Jesus Christ, the Holy Ghost, and with unwavering faith, conviction, gratitude, unconditional love for and from them I now choose to forgive myself of all events and episodes in my life that has produced within me any emotional pain, fear, hate, anger, guilt, doubt, frustration, shame, resentment, hostility, betrayal or un-forgiveness. With absolute faith, determination and irreversible willpower, I will definitely act on this crucial decision from this moment on and forever. I will definitely honor this affirmation, which will penetrate to the very depths of my soul and spirit. So be it.

AFFIRMATION # 37

With the infinite power and help of God, Jesus Christ, the Holy Ghost, and with unwavering faith, conviction, gratitude, unconditional love for and from them I now choose to have healthy, perfectly functional endocrine, immune, nervous, digestive, cardiovascular and musculoskeletal systems. With unwavering faith, determination, and irreversible willpower, I will definitely act on this crucial decision from this moment on and forever. I will definitely honor this affirmation, which will penetrate to the very depths of my soul and spirit. So be it.

AFFIRMATION # 38

With the infinite power and help of God, Jesus Christ, the Holy Ghost, and with unwavering faith, conviction, gratitude, unconditional love for and from them I now choose to magnify within me all of the elements of love such as self-reliance, self-assurance, faith, self-acceptance, self-worth, self-esteem, self-forgiveness and all other elements of unity and love. With absolute faith, determination and irreversible willpower, I will definitely act on this crucial decision from this moment on and forever. I will positively honor this affirmation, which will penetrate to the very depths of my soul and spirit. So be it.

AFFIRMATION # 39

With the infinite power and help of God, Jesus Christ, the Holy Ghost, and with unwavering faith, conviction, gratitude, unconditional love for and from them I now choose to release all beliefs that are based in the elements of disunity, fear, and hatred. With absolute faith, determination and irreversible willpower, I will definitely act on this crucial decision from this moment on and forever. I will positively honor this affirmation, which will penetrate to the very depths of my soul and spirit. So be it.

AFFIRMATION # 40

With the infinite power and help of God, Jesus Christ, the Holy Ghost, and with unwavering faith, conviction gratitude, unconditional love for me and from them, I now choose to completely heal and regenerate all of the damaged, unbalanced and dysfunctional cells, tissues, organs and systems within my body. With absolute faith, determination and irreversible willpower, I will definitely act on this crucial decision from this moment on and forever. I will positively honor this affirmation, which will penetrate to the very depths of my soul and spirit. So be it.

AFFIRMATION # 41

With the infinite power and help of God, Jesus Christ, the Holy Ghost, and with unwavering faith, conviction, gratitude, unconditional love for them and they for me. I now choose to completely release any and all need for self-pity, sympathy, love or attention that attracts to me any illness, or dysfunction of the mind and body. With absolute faith, determination and irreversible willpower, I will definitely act on this crucial decision from this moment on and forever. I will absolutely honor this affirmation, which will penetrate to the very depths of my soul and spirit. So be it.

AFFIRMATION # 42

With the infinite power and help of God, Jesus Christ, the Holy Ghost, and with unwavering faith, conviction, gratitude, unconditional love for them and they for me, I now choose to completely reject any external stimulus, micro-organism, experience or event that has produced within me any illness, disease or dysfunction. With absolute faith, determination and irreversible willpower, I will definitely act on this crucial decision from this moment on and forever. I will positively honor this affirmation, which will penetrate to the very depths of my soul and spirit. So be it.

AFFIRMATION # 43

    With the infinite power and help of God, Jesus Christ, the Holy Ghost, and with absolute faith, conviction, gratitude, unconditional love for them and they for me, I now choose eternal existence within the arms of God's love without the interference or expression of any fear based element. With absolute faith and determination I will definitely act on this crucial decision from this moment on and forever. I will positively honor this affirmation, which will penetrate to the very depths of my soul and spirit. So be it,

AFFIRMATION # 44

    With the infinite power and help of God, Jesus Christ, the Holy Ghost, and with absolute faith, conviction, gratitude, unconditional love for them and they for me, I now choose to call forth the limitless healing power of God's love to penetrate and permeate every cell, tissue, organ and system within my body, bringing me health happiness, joy and peace. With absolute faith, determination and irreversible willpower, I will definitely act on this crucial decision from this moment on and forever. I will positively honor this affirmation, which will penetrate to the very depths of my soul and spirit. So be it.

AFFIRMATION # 45

    With the infinite power and help of God, Jesus Christ, the Holy Ghost and With absolute faith, conviction, gratitude, unconditional love for them and they for me, I now choose to completely reject all sponsoring thoughts, ideas or beliefs that produce the illusion that I am separate from God and my fellow man. I am one with them, in all righteousness, and always express my creations with knowledge, wisdom, intelligence, thanksgiving and faith and with God's guidance. With absolute faith, determination and irreversible willpower I will definitely act on this crucial decision from this moment on and forever. I will positively honor this affirmation, which will penetrate to the very depths of my soul and spirit. So be it.

AFFIRMATION # 46

With the infinite power and help of God, Jesus Christ, the Holy Ghost, and with absolute faith and conviction, gratitude, unconditional love for them and they for me, I now choose to completely reject the concept of procrastination in my life. With absolute faith, determination and irreversible willpower, I will definitely act on this crucial decision from this moment on and forever. I will positively honor this affirmation, which will penetrate to the very depths of my soul and spirit. So be it

AFFIRMATION # 47

With the infinite power and help of God, Jesus Christ, the Holy Ghost, and with absolute faith, conviction, gratitude, unconditional love for them and they for me, I now choose to never again react or respond to any food sensitivities or allergies, such as meat, milk, bananas, wheat products, water additives, sugar, MSG, or any other ingested material. My immune, and digestive systems will respond to them in a normal and productive manner. With absolute faith, determination and irreversible willpower, I will now definitely act on this crucial decision from this moment on and forever. I will positively honor this affirmation, which will penetrate to the very depths of my soul and spirit. So be it.

AFFIRMATION # 48

With the infinite power and help of God, Jesus Christ, and the Holy Ghost and with absolute faith, conviction, gratitude, unconditional love for them and they for me, I now choose to reject the aging process within my body and mind. All of my cells, tissues, organs, and systems will, from this moment on, work perfectly and efficiently producing health, vitality and long life. With absolute faith, determination and irreversible willpower, I will now definitely act on this crucial decision from this moment on and forever. I will absolutely honor this affirmation, which will penetrate to the very depths of my soul and spirit. So be it.

AFFIRFMATION # 49

With the infinite power and help of God, Jesus Christ, the Holy Ghost, and with absolute faith conviction gratitude, unconditional love for them and they for me, I now choose to create for me abundance and prosperity always to be used righteously and productively. With absolute faith, determination and irreversible willpower, I will now definitely act on this crucial decision from this moment on and forever. I will absolutely honor this affirmation, which will penetrate to the very depths of my soul and spirit. So be it.

AFFIRMATION # 50

With the infinite power and help of God, Jesus Christ, the Holy Ghost, and with absolute faith, conviction, gratitude, unconditional love for them and they for me, I now choose to reject all of the causes of my allergies and food sensitivities. With absolute faith, determination and irreversible willpower, I will definitely act on this crucial decision from this moment on and forever. I will positively honor this affirmation, which will penetrate to the very depths of my soul and spirit. So be it

AFFIRMATION # 51

With the infinite power and help of God, Jesus Christ, the Holy Ghost, and with absolute faith, conviction, gratitude, unconditional love for them and they for me, I now choose to seek for true knowledge, wisdom and intelligence to better serve God and my fellow man and ultimately to glorify Him. With absolute faith, determination and irreversible willpower, I will definitely act on this crucial decision from this moment on and forever. I will positively honor this affirmation, which will penetrate to the very depths of my soul and spirit. So be it.

AFFIRMATION # 52

With the infinite power and help of God, Jesus Christ, the Holy Ghost, and with absolute faith, conviction, gratitude, unconditional love for them and they for me, I now choose to expunge and erase all bigotry from my mind and my actions. I will never again express it to another human being. With absolute faith, determination and irreversible willpower, I will now definitely act on this crucial decision from this moment on and forever. I will positively honor this affirmation, which will penetrate to the very depths of my soul and spirit. So be it.

Chapter Eight

YET ANOTHER FORMAT FOR AFFIRMATIONS

AFFIRMATION # 1

WITH THE WONDERFULLY, INFINITE POWER and help of God, Jesus Christ, the Holy Ghost, and with absolute thanksgiving and unconditional love for them and they for me, and with intense power and conviction I now choose the beautiful experience of continually increasing my mental and physical abilities and to access my memory much easier. Nothing will interfere with this decision now and forever, it is final. I will positively honor this affirmation, which will penetrate to the very depths of my soul and spirit. So be it.

AFFIRMATION # 2

With the wonderfully, infinite power and help of God, Jesus Christ, the Holy Ghost, and with absolute gratitude, thanksgiving and unconditional love for them and they for me and with intense power and conviction I now choose the beautiful experience of knowing absolutely that these creative affirmations will bring me health, happiness, joy, and peace. They are now deeply imbedded and registered in my mind and will be extremely effective in accomplishing their aim. Nothing will interfere with this decision now and forever. It is final. I will positively honor this affirmation, which will penetrate to the very depths of my soul and spirit. So be it.

AFFIRMATION # 3

With the wonderfully, infinite power and help of God, Jesus Christ, the Holy Ghost and with absolute gratitude, and unconditional love for them and they for me, and with intense power and conviction I now choose the beautiful experience of completely releasing any and all need for sympathy, love or attention that draws to me any illness or dysfunction of my mind or body. Nothing will interfere with this decision, now and forever. It is final. I will positively honor this affirmation, which will penetrate to the very depths of my soul and spirit. So be it.

AFFIRMATION # 4

With the wonderfully, infinite power and help of God, Jesus Christ, The Holy Ghost, and with absolute gratitude, and unconditional love for them and they for me and with intense power and conviction I now choose the beautiful experience of forgiving everyone for all of the things they have said or done that has produced within me any anger, fear, guilt, shame, hate, frustration, resentment or any other destructive trait. Nothing will interfere with this decision, now and forever. It is final. I will positively honor this affirmation, which will penetrate to the very depths of my soul and spirit. So be it.

AFFIRMATION # 5

With the wonderfully, infinite power and help of God, Jesus Christ, the Holy Ghost and with absolute gratitude, and unconditional love for them and they for me, and with intense power and conviction I now choose the beautiful experience of forgiving anyone in authority for anything they have said or done that has produced in my life, any anger, fear, guilt, shame, hate, frustration, resentment or any other destructive, unrighteous trait. Nothing will interfere with this decision, now and forever. It is final. I will positively honor this affirmation, which will penetrate to the very depths of my soul and spirit. So be it.

AFFIRMATION # 6

With the wonderfully, infinite power and help of God, Jesus Christ, the Holy Ghost and with absolute gratitude, and unconditional love for them and they for me, and with intense power and conviction I now choose the beautiful experience of forgiving myself for all of the things I have said or done, that has brought distress or pain to me or anyone else. Nothing will interfere with this decision. It is final. I will positively honor this affirmation, which will penetrate to the very depths of my soul and spirit. So be it.

AFFIRMATION # 7

With the wonderfully, infinite power and help of God, Jesus Christ, the Holy Ghost and with absolute gratitude, and unconditional love for them and they for me I now choose the beautiful experience of releasing and rejecting all of the destructive fears and unrighteous traits that has produced any illness, disease or impairment of my mind or body. Nothing will interfere with this decision. It is final. I will positively honor this affirmation, which will penetrate to the very depths of my soul and spirit. So be it.

AFFIRMATION # 8

With the wonderfully infinite power and help of God, Jesus Christ, the Holy Ghost and with absolute gratitude, and unconditional love for them and they for me I now choose the beautiful experience of forgiving all events in my life that has caused any worry, un-forgiveness, resentment or feelings of betrayal, mental pain or illness. Nothing will interfere with this decision. It is final. I will positively honor this affirmation, which will penetrate to the very depths of my soul and spirit. So be it.

AFFIRMATION # 9

With the wonderfully, infinite power and help of God, Jesus Christ, the Holy Ghost, and with absolute gratitude, and unconditional love for them and they for me, I now choose the beautiful experience of continually attracting the healing powers of God, and Christ, which will penetrate and permeate every cell within my body, and return me to health and vitality. Nothing will interfere with this decision. It is final. I will positively honor this affirmation, which will penetrate to the very depths of my soul and spirit. So be it.

Chapter Nine

RIGHTEOUS AFFIRMATIONS

AFFIRMATION # 1

WITH THE AMAZING HELP OF God, Jesus Christ, the Holy Ghost and with intense power, absolute conviction, gratitude, and unconditional love for them and they for me, I now choose to forgive my brothers and sisters for everything they have ever said or done that has produced, within me, any anger, fear, guilt, shame, hate, frustration, resentment, or any other destructive emotion. With complete faith, determination and irreversible willpower I will now definitely act on this crucial decision from this moment on and forever. So be it.

AFFIRMATION # 2

With the amazing help of God, Jesus Christ, the Holy Ghost and with intense power, absolute conviction, gratitude, and unconditional love for them and they for me, I now choose to forgive my parents for all of the things they have said or done that has produced within me any anger, fear, guilt, shame, hate, frustration, resentment, or any other destructive emotion. With complete faith, determination and irreversible willpower, I will now definitely act on this crucial decision from this moment on and forever. So be it.

AFFIRMATION # 3

With the infinite power and help of God, Jesus Christ, The Holy Ghost, and with absolute faith, gratitude, conviction, unconditional love for them and they for me, I now choose to create for me a body and mind that is completely free of all illness, allergies, food sensitivities, dysfunctions, degeneration of cells and pain. With complete faith, determination and irreversible willpower, I will now definitely act on this crucial decision from this moment on and forever. So be it.

AFFIRMATION # 4

With the infinite power and help of God, Jesus Christ, the Holy Ghost, and with absolute faith, gratitude, conviction, and unconditional love for them and they for me, I now choose to create a forgiveness for all experiences and events in my life that has produced any emotional pain, fear, hate, anger, guilt, shame, resentment or un-forgiveness for myself and others. With complete faith, determination and irreversible willpower, I will now definitely act on this crucial decision from this moment on and forever. So be it.

AFFIRMATION # 5

With the infinite power and help of God, Jesus Christ, the Holy Ghost, and with absolute faith, gratitude, conviction, and unconditional love for them and they for me, I now choose to create spiritual and physical abundance, prosperity and joy for me and my family. With complete faith, determination and irreversible willpower, I will now definitely act on this crucial decision from this moment on and forever. So be it.

AFFIRMATION # 6

With the infinite power and help of God, Jesus Christ, the holy Ghost, and with absolute faith, gratitude, conviction, and unconditional love for them and they for me, I now choose to create for me a complete release of all beliefs that are based on disunity, unrighteousness, fear and hate. With complete faith, determination and irreversible willpower, I will now definitely act on this crucial decision from this moment on and forever. So be it.

AFFIRMATION # 7

With the infinite power and help of God, Jesus Christ, the Holy Ghost, and with absolute faith, gratitude, Conviction, and unconditional love for them and they for me I now choose to create for me a healthy nervous system that will function at maximum efficiency at all levels and times. With compete faith, determination and irreversible willpower; I will now definitely act on this crucial decision from this moment on and forever. So be it.

AFFIRMATION # 8

With the infinite power and help of God, Jesus Christ, the Holy Ghost, and with absolute faith, gratitude, conviction, and unconditional love for them and they for me I now choose to create for me the ability to call forth the great healing powers of heaven which will penetrate and permeate every cell within my mind and body. With complete faith, determination and irreversible willpower, I will now definitely act on this crucial decision from this moment on and forever. So be it.

AFFIRMATION # 9

With the infinite power and help of God the Father, Jesus Christ, the Holy Ghost, and with intense gratitude, thankfulness and unconditional love for them and they for me, I now choose to be completely free of _____, and all other ailments. (Add any illness or ailment you desire in the blank space) I will now definitely act on this affirmation irrefutably and with complete faith, determination, irreversible willpower, and love, from this moment on and forever. So be it.

AFFIRMATION # 10

With the infinite power and help of God, Jesus Christ, the Holy Ghost, and with intense gratitude, and unconditional love for them and they me, I now choose to be completely pain free in all parts of my body. With complete faith, determination and irreversible willpower, I will now definitely act on this affirmation with irrefutable faith and irreversible willpower from this moment on and forever. So be it.

Chapter Ten

MORE RIGHTEOUS AFFIRMATIONS

THIS CHAPTER OF AFFIRMATIONS WILL embrace the perfecting of many of the righteous elements of unity, such as love, humility, faith etc.

The righteous elements of unity are those that must be perfected as much as possible in this life, in order to reside with God again. The unrighteous elements in this chapter, which are those, of disunity, which must all be expunged from our bodies and minds before we can gain God's presence.

There are many other elements of both unity and disunity that should be researched, embraced or expunged. In all, there are about two hundred of each that need to be addressed. To find and research each of these elements will be up to the reader. These are the elements that when expunged or embraced will constitutes much of the pathway to perfection and God's kingdom. Consider this pathway to be a journey, both in this life and during the millennium.

Matt. 5:48: Be ye, therefore perfect even as your Father who is in heaven is perfect. (This is God's commandment, pure and simple.) Since this commandment cannot be completely fulfilled in this life it must be a journey that lasts through the millennium. This doesn't mean that we should put off, until the millennium to do the best we can to obey this commandment in this life.

AFFIRMATION # 1

With the infinite power and help of God, Jesus Christ, the Holy Ghost, and with intense gratitude, faith, and unconditional love for them and they for me, I now choose to embrace and perfect the element of appreciation for the rest of my life. I will now definitely act on this crucial affirmation from this moment on and forever. This affirmation will penetrate to the very depths of my soul and spirit. So be it.

AFFIRMATION # 2

With the infinite power and help of God, Jesus Christ, the Holy Ghost, and with intense faith, gratitude, and unconditional love for them and they for me, I now choose to embrace and perfect the righteous trait of inner beauty for the rest of my life. I will now definitely act on this essential affirmation from this moment on and forever. This affirmation will penetrate to the very depths of my soul and spirit. So be it.

AFFIRMATION # 3

With the infinite power and help of God, Jesus Christ, the Holy Ghost, and with intense faith, gratitude, and unconditional love for them and they for me, I now choose to embrace and perfect the element of benevolence for the rest of my life. I will now definitely act on this crucial affirmation from this moment on and forever. This affirmation will penetrate to the very depths of my soul and spirit. So be it.

AFFIRMATION # 4

With the infinite power and help of God, Jesus Christ, the Holy Ghost, and with intense faith, gratitude, and unconditional love for them and they for me, I now choose to embrace and perfect the element of charity for the rest of my life. I will now definitely act on this crucial affirmation from this moment on and forever. This affirmation will penetrate to the very depths of my soul and spirit. So be it.

AFFIRMATION # 5

With the infinite power and help of God, Jesus Christ, the Holy Ghost, and with intense faith, gratitude, and unconditional love for them and they for me, I now choose to embrace and perfect the element of commitment for the rest of my life. I will now definitely act on this crucial affirmation from this moment on and forever. This affirmation will penetrate to the very depths of my soul and spirit. So be it.

AFFIRMATION # 6

With the infinite power and help of God, Jesus Christ, the Holy Ghost, and with intense faith, gratitude, and unconditional love for them and they for me, I now choose to embrace and perfect the righteous element of compassion for the rest of my life. I will now definitely act on this crucial affirmation from this moment on and forever. This affirmation will penetrate to the very depths of my soul and spirit. So be it.

AFFIRMATION # 7

With the infinite power and help of God, Jesus Christ, the Holy Ghost, and with intense faith, gratitude, and unconditional love for them and they for me, I now choose to embrace and perfect the righteous element of confidence for the rest of my life. I will now definitely act on this crucial affirmation from this moment on and forever. This affirmation will penetrate to the very depths of my soul and spirit. So be it.

AFFIRMATION # 8

With the infinite power and help of God, Jesus Christ, the Holy Ghost, and with intense faith, gratitude, and unconditional love for them and they for me I now choose to embrace and perfect the righteous element of consideration for the rest of my life. I will now definitely act on this crucial affirmation from this moment on and forever. This affirmation will penetrate to the very depths of my soul and spirit. So be it.

AFFIRMATION # 9

With the infinite power and help of God, Jesus Christ, the Holy Ghost, and with intense faith, gratitude, and unconditional love for them and they for me, I now choose to embrace and perfect the righteous element of consistency for the rest of my life. I will now definitely act on this crucial affirmation from this moment on and forever. This affirmation will penetrate to the very depths of my soul and spirit. So be it.

AFFIRMATION # 10

With the infinite power and help of God, Jesus Christ, the Holy Ghost, and with intense faith, gratitude, and unconditional love for them and they for me, I now choose to embrace and perfect the righteous element of courage for the rest of my life. I will now definitely act on this crucial affirmation from this moment on and forever. This affirmation will penetrate to the very depths of my soul and spirit. So be it.

AFFIRMATION # 11

With the infinite power and help of God, Jesus Christ, the Holy Ghost, and with intense faith, gratitude, and unconditional love for them and they for me, I now choose to embrace and perfect the righteous element of creativity for the rest of my life. I will now definitely act on this crucial affirmation from this moment on and forever. This affirmation will penetrate to the very depths of my soul and spirit. So be it.

AFFIRMATION # 12

With the infinite power and help of God, Jesus Christ, the Holy Ghost, and with intense faith, gratitude, thankfulness, and unconditional love for them and they for me, I now choose to embrace and perfect the righteous element of dedication for the rest of my life. I will now definitely act on this crucial affirmation from this moment on and forever. This affirmation will penetrate to the very depths f my soul and spirit. So be it.

AFFIRMATION # 13

With the infinite power and help of god, Jesus Christ, the Holy Ghost, and with intense faith, gratitude, and unconditional love for them, and they for me, I now choose to embrace and perfect the righteous element of discernment for the rest of my life. I will now definitely act on this crucial affirmation from this moment on and forever. This affirmation will penetrate to the very depths of my soul and spirit. So be it.

AFFIRMATION # 14

With the infinite power and help of God, Jesus Christ, the Holy Ghost, and with intense faith, gratitude, and unconditional love for them and they for me, I now choose to embrace and perfect the righteous element of durability for the rest of my life. I will now definitely act on this crucial affirmation from this moment on and forever. This affirmation will penetrate to the very depths of my soul and spirit. So be it.

AFFIRMATION # 15

With the infinite power and help of God, Jesus Christ, the Holy Ghost, and with intense faith, gratitude, and unconditional love for them and they for me, I now choose to embrace and perfect the righteous element of empathy for the rest of my life. I will now definitely act on this crucial affirmation from this moment on and forever. This affirmation will penetrate to the very depths of my soul and spirit. So be it.

AFFIRMATION # 16

With the infinite power and help of God, Jesus Christ, the Holy Ghost, and with intense faith, gratitude, and unconditional love for them and they for me, I now choose to embrace and perfect the righteous element of equality for the rest of my life. I will now definitely act on this crucial affirmation from this moment on and forever. This affirmation will penetrate to the very depths of my soul and spirit. So be it.

AFFIRMATION # 17

With the infinite power and help of God, Jesus Christ, the Holy Ghost, and with intense faith, gratitude, and unconditional love for them and they for me, I now choose to embrace and perfect the righteous element of endurance for the rest of my life. I will now definitely act on this righteous affirmation from this moment on and forever. This affirmation will penetrate to the very depths of my soul and spirit. So be it.

AFFIRMATION # 18

With the infinite power and help of God, Jesus Christ, the Holy Ghost, and with intense faith, gratitude, and unconditional love for them and they for me, I now choose to embrace and perfect the righteous element of forgiveness for the rest my life. I will now definitely act on this crucial affirmation from this moment on and forever. This affirmation will penetrate to the very depths of my soul and spirit. So be it.

AFFIRMATION # 19

With the infinite power and help of God, Jesus Christ, the Holy Ghost, and with intense faith, Gratitude, and unconditional love for them and they for me, I now choose to embrace and perfect the righteous element of friendliness for the rest of my life. I will now definitely act on this crucial affirmation from this moment on and forever. This affirmation will penetrate to the very depths of my soul and spirit. So be it.

AFFIRMTION # 20

With the infinite power and help of God, Jesus Christ, the Holy Ghost, and with intense faith, gratitude, and unconditional love for them and they for me, I now choose to embrace and perfect the righteous element of gentleness for the rest of my life. I will now definitely act on this crucial affirmation from this moment on and forever. This affirmation will penetrate to the very depths of my soul and spirit. So be it.

AFFIRMATION # 21

With the infinite power and help of God, Jesus Christ, the Holy Ghost, and with intense faith, gratitude, and unconditional love for them and they for me, I now choose to embrace and perfect the righteous element of helpfulness, for the rest of my life. I will now definitely act on this crucial affirmation from this moment on and forever. This affirmation will penetrate to the very depths of my soul and spirit. So be it.

AFFIRMATION # 22

With the infinite power and help of God, Jesus Christ, the Holy Ghost, and with intense faith, gratitude, and unconditional love for them and they for me, I now choose to embrace and perfect the righteous element of honesty for the rest of my life. I will now definitely act on this crucial affirmation from this moment on and forever. This affirmation will penetrate to the very depths of my soul and spirit. So be it.

AFFIRMATION # 23

With the infinite power and help of God, Jesus Christ, the Holy Ghost, and with intense faith, gratitude, and unconditional love for them and they for me, I now choose to embrace and perfect the righteous element of honor for the rest of my life. I will now definitely act on this crucial affirmation from now on and forever. This affirmation will penetrate to the very depths of my soul and spirit. So be it.

AFFIRMATION # 24

With the infinite power and help of God, Jesus Christ, the Holy Ghost, and with intense faith, gratitude, and unconditional love for them and they for me, I now choose to embrace and perfect the righteous element of hope for the rest of my life. I will now definitely act on this crucial affirmation from this moment on and forever. This affirmation will penetrate to the very depths of my soul and spirit. So be it.

AFFIRMATION # 25

With the infinite power and help of God, Jesus Christ, the Holy Ghost, and with intense faith, gratitude, and unconditional love for them and they for me, I now choose to embrace and perfect the righteous element of humility for the rest of my life. I will now definitely act on this crucial affirmation from this moment on and forever. This affirmation will penetrate to the very depths of my soul and spirit. So be it.

AFFIRMATION # 26

With the infinite power and help of God, Jesus Christ, the Holy Ghost, and with intense faith, gratitude, and unconditional love for them and they for me, I now choose to embrace and perfect the righteous element of humor for the rest of my life. I will now definitely act on this crucial affirmation from this moment on and forever. This affirmation will penetrate to the very depths of my soul and spirit. So be it.

AFFIRMATION # 27

With the infinite power and help of God, Jesus Christ, the Holy Ghost, and with intense faith, gratitude, and unconditional love for them and they for me, I now choose to embrace and perfect the righteous element of industry for the rest of my life. I will now definitely act on this crucial affirmation from this moment on and forever. This affirmation will penetrate to the very depths of my soul and spirit. So be it.

AFFIRMATION # 28

With the infinite power and help of God, Jesus Christ, the Holy Ghost, and with intense faith, gratitude, and unconditional love for them and they for me, I now choose to embrace and perfect the righteous element of inquisitiveness for the rest of my life. I will now definitely act on this crucial affirmation from this moment on and forever. This affirmation will penetrate to the very depths of my soul and spirit. So be it.

AFFIRMATION # 29

With the infinite power and help of God, Jesus Christ, the Holy Ghost, and with intense faith, gratitude, and unconditional love for them and they for me, I now choose to embrace and perfect the righteous element of integrity for the rest of my life. I will now definitely act on this crucial affirmation from this moment on and forever. This affirmation will penetrate to the very depths of my soul and spirit. So be it.

AFFIRMATION # 30

With the infinite power and help of God, Jesus Christ, the Holy Ghost, and with intense faith, gratitude, and unconditional love for them and they for me, I now choose to embrace and perfect the righteous element of intention for the rest of my life. I will now definitely act on this crucial affirmation from this moment on and forever. This affirmation will penetrate to the very depths of my soul and spirit. So be it.

AFFIRMATION # 31

With the infinite power and help of God, Jesus Christ, the Holy Ghost, and with intense faith, gratitude, and unconditional love for them and they for me, I now choose to embrace and perfect the righteous element of justice for the rest of my life. I will now definitely act on this crucial affirmation from this moment on and forever. This affirmation will penetrate to the very depths of my soul and spirit. So be it.

AFFIRMATION # 32

With the infinite power and help of God, Jesus Christ, the Holy Ghost, and with intense faith, gratitude, and unconditional love for them and they for me, I now choose to embrace and perfect, the righteous element of kindness for the rest of my life. I will now definitely act on this crucial affirmation from this moment on and forever. This affirmation will penetrate to the very depths of my soul and spirit. So be it.

AFFIRMATION # 33

With the infinite power and help of God, Jesus Christ, the Holy Ghost, and with intense faith, gratitude, and unconditional love for them and they for me, I now choose to embrace and perfect the righteous element of knowledge for the rest of my life. I will now definitely act on this crucial affirmation from this moment on and forever. This affirmation will penetrate to the very depths of my soul and spirit. So be it.

AFFIRMATION # 34

With the infinite power and help of God, Jesus Christ, the Holy Ghost, and with intense faith, gratitude, and unconditional love for them and they for me, I now choose to embrace and perfect the righteous element of love for the rest of my life. I will now definitely act on this crucial affirmation for the rest of my life and forever. This affirmation will penetrate to the very depths of my soul and spirit. So be it.

AFFIRMATION # 35

With the infinite power and help of God, Jesus Christ, the Holy Ghost, and with intense faith, gratitude, and unconditional love for them and they for me, I now choose to embrace and perfect the righteous element of loyalty for the rest of my life. I will now definitely act on this crucial affirmation from this moment on and forever. This affirmation will penetrate to the very depths of my soul and spirit. So be it.

AFFIRMATION # 36

With the infinite power and help of God, Jesus Christ, the Holy Ghost, and with intense faith, gratitude, and unconditional love for them and they for me, I now choose to embrace and perfect the righteous element of meekness for the rest of my life. I will now definitely act on this crucial affirmation from this moment on and forever. This affirmation will penetrate to the very depths of my soul and spirit. So be it.

AFFIRMATION # 37

With the infinite power and help of God, Jesus Christ, the Holy Ghost, and with intense faith, gratitude, and unconditional love for them and they for me, I now choose to embrace and perfect the righteous element of mercy for the rest of my life. I will now definitely act on this crucial affirmation from this moment on and forever. This affirmation will penetrate to the very depths of my soul and spirit. So be it.

AFFIRMATION # 38

With the infinite power and help of God, Jesus Christ, the Holy Ghost, and with intense faith, gratitude, and unconditional love for them and they for me, I now choose to embrace and perfect the righteous element of modesty for the rest of my life. I will now definitely act on this crucial affirmation from this moment on and forever. This affirmation will penetrate to the very depths f my soul and spirit. So be it.

AFFIRMATION # 39

With the infinite power and help of God, Jesus Christ, the Holy Ghost, and with intense faith, gratitude, and unconditional love for them and they for me, I now choose to embrace and perfect the righteous element of morality for the rest of my life. I will now definitely act on this crucial affirmation from this moment on and forever. This affirmation will penetrate to the very depths of my soul and spirit. So be it.

AFFIRMATION # 40

With the infinite power and help of God, Jesus Christ, the Holy Ghost, and with intense faith, gratitude, and unconditional love for them and they for me, I now choose to embrace and perfect the righteous element of motivation for the rest of my life. I will now definitely act on this crucial affirmation from this moment on and forever. This affirmation will penetrate to the very depths f my soul and spirit. So be it

AFFIRMATION # 41

With the infinite power and help of God, Jesus Christ, the Holy Ghost, and with intense faith, gratitude, and unconditional love for them and they for me, I now choose to embrace and perfect the righteous element of obedience for the rest of my life. I will now definitely act on this crucial affirmation from this moment on and forever. This affirmation will penetrate to the very depths of my soul and spirit. So be it.

AFFIRMATION # 42

With the infinite power and help of God, Jesus Christ, the Holy Ghost, and with intense faith, gratitude, and unconditional love for them and they for me, I now choose to embrace and perfect the righteous element of patience for the rest of my life. I will now definitely act on this crucial affirmation from this moment on and forever. This affirmation will penetrate to the very depths of my soul and spirit. So be it.

AFFIRMATION # 43

With the infinite power and help of God, Jesus Christ, the Holy Ghost, and with intense faith, gratitude, and unconditional love for them and they for me, I now choose to embrace and perfect the righteous element of persistence for the rest of my life. I will now definitely act on this crucial affirmation from this moment on and forever. This affirmation will penetrate to the very depths of my soul and spirit. So be it.

AFFIRMATION # 44

With the infinite power and help of God, Jesus Christ, the Holy Ghost, and with intense faith, gratitude, and unconditional love for them and they for me, I now choose to embrace and perfect the righteous element of purity, for the rest of my life. I will now definitely act on this crucial affirmation from this moment on and forever. This affirmation will penetrate to the very depths of my heart and soul. So be it.

AFFIRMATION # 45

With the infinite power and help of God, Jesus Christ, the Holy Ghost, and with intense faith, gratitude, and unconditional love for them and they for me, I now choose to embrace and perfect, the righteous element of responsibility for the rest of my life. I will now definitely act on this crucial affirmation from this moment on and forever. This affirmation will penetrate to the very depths of my heart and soul. So be it.

AFFIRMATION # 46

With the infinite power and help of God, Jesus Christ, the Holy Ghost, and with intense faith, gratitude, and unconditional love for them and they for me, I now choose to embrace and perfect the righteous element of reverence, for the rest of my life. I will now definitely act on this crucial affirmation from this moment on and forever. This affirmation will penetrate to the very heart and soul. So be it.

AFFIRMATION # 47

With the infinite power and help of God, Jesus Christ, the Holy Ghost, and with intense faith gratitude, and unconditional love for them and they for me, I now choose to embrace and perfect the righteous element of sacrifice for the rest of my life. I will now definitely act on this crucial decision from this moment on and forever. This affirmation will penetrate to the very heart and soul. So be it.

AFFIRMATION # 48

With the infinite power and help of God, Jesus Christ, the Holy Ghost, and with intense, faith, gratitude, and unconditional love for them and they me, I now choose to embrace and perfect the righteous element of self-esteem for the rest of my life. I will now definitely act on this crucial affirmation from this moment on and forever. This affirmation will penetrate to the very depths of my heart and soul. So be it.

AFFIRMATION # 49

With the infinite power and help of God, Jesus Christ, the Holy Ghost, and with intense faith, gratitude, and unconditional love for them and they for me, I now choose to embrace and perfect the righteous element of self-reliance for the rest of my life. I will now definitely act on this crucial affirmation from this moment on and forever. This affirmation will penetrate to the very depths of my heart and soul. So be **it.**

AFFIRMATION # 50

With the infinite power and help of God, Jesus Christ, the Holy Ghost, and with intense faith, gratitude, and unconditional love for them and they for me, I now choose to embrace and perfect the righteous element of sensitivity for the rest of my life. I will definitely act on this crucial affirmation from this moment on and forever. This affirmation will penetrate to the very depths of my heart and soul. So be it.

AFFIRMATION # 51

With the infinite power and help of God, Jesus Christ, the Holy Ghost, and with intense faith, Gratitude, and unconditional love for them and they for me, I now choose to embrace and perfect, the righteous element of spirituality for the rest of my life. I will now definitely act on this crucial affirmation from this moment on and forever. This affirmation will penetrate to the very depths of my heart and soul. So be it.

AFFIRMATION # 52

With the infinite power and help of God, Jesus Christ, the Holy Ghost, and with intense faith, gratitude, and unconditional love for them and they for me, I now choose to embrace and perfect the righteous element of strength, for the rest of my life. I will now definitely act on this crucial affirmation from this moment on and forever. This affirmation will penetrate to the very depths of my heart and soul. So be it.

AFFIRMATION # 53

With the infinite power and help of God, Jesus Christ, the Holy Ghost, and with intense faith, gratitude, and unconditional love for them and they for me, I now choose to embrace and perfect the righteous element of success for the rest of my life. I will now definitely act on this crucial affirmation from this moment on and forever. This affirmation will penetrate to the very depths of my heart and soul. So be it.

AFFIRMATION # 54

With the infinite power and help of God, Jesus Christ, the Holy Ghost, and with intense faith, gratitude, and unconditional love for them and they for me, I now choose to embrace and perfect the righteous element of temperance for the rest of my life. I will now definitely act on this crucial affirmation from this moment on and forever. This affirmation will penetrate to the very depths of my heart and soul. So be it.

AFFIRMATION # 55

With the infinite power and help of God, Jesus Christ, the Holy Ghost, and with intense faith, gratitude, and unconditional love for them and they for me, I now choose to embrace and perfect the righteous element of tolerance for the rest of my life. I will now definitely act on this crucial affirmation from this moment on and forever. This affirmation will penetrate to the very depths of my heart and soul. So be it.

AFFIRMATION # 56

With the infinite power and help of God, Jesus Christ, the Holy Ghost, and with intense faith, gratitude, and unconditional love for them and they for me, I now choose to embrace and perfect the righteous element of trust for the rest of my life. I will now definitely act on this crucial affirmation from this moment on and forever. This affirmation will penetrate to the very depths of my heart and soul. So be it.

AFFIRMATION # 57

With the infinite power and help of God, Jesus Christ, the Holy Ghost, and with intense faith, gratitude, and unconditional love for them and they for me, I now choose to embrace and perfect the righteous element of virtue for the rest of my life. I will now definitely act on this crucial affirmation from this moment on and forever. This affirmation will penetrate to the very depths of my heart and soul. So be it.

There are many more righteous elements that need perfecting. These I have chosen because they are the ones I need to work on. It is up to you to go through the dictionary and choose those righteous elements that pertain to you. In my estimation, whatever you do, choose one of the formats I have chosen, or if you wish create one of your own, make sure it includes Deity in all of the units you choose.

Chapter Eleven

EVEN MORE UNRIGHTEOUS AFFIRMATIONS

AFFIRMATION # 1

WITH THE INFINITE POWER AND help of God, Jesus Christ, the Holy Ghost, and with intense faith, gratitude, and unconditional love for them and they for me, I now choose to purge the unrighteous element of anger, from my emotions and life forever. I will now act on this very essential affirmation from this moment on and for eternity. This affirmation will penetrate to the very depths of my heart and soul. So be it.

AFFIRMATIONS # 2

With the infinite power and help of God, Jesus Christ. The Holy Ghost, and with intense faith gratitude, and unconditional love for them and they for me I now choose to purge the unrighteous element of apathy from my emotions and life forever. I will now act on this very essential affirmation from this moment on and for eternity. This affirmation will penetrate to the very depths of my heart and soul. So be it.

AFFIRMATION # 3

With the infinite power and help of God, Jesus Christ, the Holy Ghost, and with intense faith, gratitude, and unconditional love for them and they for me I now choose to purge the unrighteous element of avarice from my emotions and my life forever. I will now act on this very essential affirmation from this moment on and for eternity. This affirmation will penetrate to the very depths of my heart and soul. So be it.

AFFIRMATIONS # 4

With the infinite power and help of God, Jesus Christ, the Holy Ghost, and with intense faith, gratitude, and unconditional love for them and they for me I now choose to purge the unrighteous element of bigotry from my thoughts and actions forever. I will now act on this very essential affirmation from this moment on and for eternity. This affirmation will penetrate to the very depths of my heart and soul. So be it.

AFFIRMATION # 5

With the infinite power and help of God, Jesus Christ, the Holy Ghost, and with intense faith, gratitude, and unconditional love for them and they for me, I now choose to purge the unrighteous element of cheating from my thoughts and actions and my life. I will now act on this very essential affirmation from this moment on and for eternity. This affirmation will penetrate to the very depths of my heart and soul. So be it.

AFFIRMATION # 6

With the infinite power and help of God, Jesus Christ, the Holy Ghost, and with intense faith, gratitude, and unconditional love for them and they for me I now choose to purge the unrighteous element of contempt from my actions and my life forever. I will now act on his very essential affirmation from this moment on and for eternity. This affirmation will penetrate to the very depths of my heart and soul. So be it.

AFFIRMATION # 7

With the infinite power and help of God, Jesus Christ, the Holy Ghost, and with intense faith, gratitude, and unconditional love for them and they for me, I now choose to purge the unrighteous element of contention from my actions and my life forever. I will now act on this very essential affirmation from this moment on and for eternity. This affirmation will penetrate to the very depths of my heart and soul. So be it.

AFFIRMATION # 8

With the infinite power and help of God, Jesus Christ, the Holy Ghost, and with intense faith, gratitude, and unconditional love for them and they for me, I now choose to purge the unrighteous trait of controlling others from my actions and my life forever. I will now act on this very essential affirmation from this moment on and for eternity. This affirmation will penetrate to the very depths of my heart and soul. So be it.

AFFIRMATION # 9

With the infinite power and help of God, Jesus Christ, the Holy Ghost, and with intense faith, gratitude, and unconditional love for them and they for me, I now choose to purge the unrighteous element of cowardice from my actions and from my life forever. I will now act on this very essential affirmation from this moment on and for eternity. This affirmation will penetrate to the very depths of my heart and soul. So be it.

AFFORMATION # 10

With the infinite power and help of God, Jesus Christ, the Holy Ghost, and with intense faith, gratitude, and unconditional love for them and they for me, I now choose to purge the unrighteous element of cruelty from my actions and from my life forever. I will now act on this very essential affirmation from this moment on and for eternity. This affirmation will penetrate to the very depths of my heart and soul. So be it.

AFFIRMATION # 11

With the infinite power and help of God, Jesus Christ, the Holy Ghost, and with intense faith, gratitude, and unconditional love for them and they for me, I now choose to purge the unrighteous element of devilishness from my thoughts and actions from my life forever. I will now definitely act on this very essential affirmation for eternity. So be it.

AFFIRMATION # 12

With the infinite power and help of God, Jesus Christ, the Holy Ghost, and with intense faith, gratitude, and unconditional love for them and they for me, I now choose to purge the unrighteous element of dishonesty from my thoughts and actions and from my life forever. I will now act on this very essential affirmation for eternity. This affirmation will penetrate to the very depths of my heart and soul. So be it.

AFFIRMATION # 13

With the infinite power and help of God, Jesus Christ, the Holy Ghost, and with intense faith, gratitude, and unconditional love for them and they for me. I now choose to purge the unrighteous element of disloyalty from my thoughts and actions from my life forever. I will now act on this very essential affirmation for eternity. This affirmation will penetrate to the very depths of my heart and soul. So be it

AFFIRMATION # 14

With the infinite power and help of God, Jesus Christ, the Holy Ghost, and with intense faith, gratitude, and unconditional love for them and they for me, I now choose to purge the unrighteous element of disobedience from my thoughts and actions forever. I will now act on this very essential affirmation from this moment on and for eternity. This affirmation will penetrate to the very depths of my heart and soul. So be it.

AFFIRMATION # 15

With the infinite power and help of God, Jesus Christ, the Holy Ghost, and with intense, faith, gratitude, and unconditional love for them and they for me, I now choose to purge the unrighteous element of distain from my thoughts and actions forever. I will now act on this very essential affirmation from this moment on and for eternity. This affirmation will penetrate to the very depths of my heart and soul. So be it.

AFFIRMATION # 16

With the infinite power and help of God Jesus Christ, the Holy Ghost, and with intense faith, gratitude, and unconditional love for them and they for me, I now choose to purge the unrighteous element of doubt from my thoughts and actions forever. I will now act on this very essential affirmation from this moment on and for eternity. This affirmation will penetrate to the very depths of my heart and soul. So be it.

AFFIRMATION # 17

With the infinite power and help of God, Jesus Christ, the Holy Ghost, and with intense faith, gratitude, and unconditional love for them and they for me I now choose to purge the unrighteous element of envy from my thoughts and actions forever. I will now act on this very essential affirmation from this moment on and for eternity. This affirmation will penetrate to the very depths of my heart and soul. So be it.

AFFIRMATION # 18

With the infinite power and help of God, Jesus Christ, the Holy Ghost, and with intense faith, gratitude, and unconditional love for them and they for me, I now choose to purge the unrighteous trait of evil-mindedness from my thoughts and actions forever, I will now act on this very essential affirmation from this moment on and for eternity. This affirmation will penetrate to the very depths of my heart and soul. So be it.

AFFIRMATION # 19

With the infinite power and help of God, Jesus Christ, the Holy Ghost, and with intense faith, gratitude, and unconditional love for them and they for me, I now choose to purge the unrighteous trait of conceding or giving-up without a fight. I will now act on this very essential affirmation from this moment on and for eternity. This affirmation will penetrate to the very depths of my heart and soul. So be it.

DR. LAUREN J. BALL

AFFIRMATION # 20

With the infinite power and help of God, Jesus Christ, the Holy Ghost, and with intense faith, gratitude, and unconditional love for them and they for me, I now choose to purge the unrighteous trait of gossiping from now on and forever. I will now act on this very essential affirmation from this moment on and for eternity. This affirmation will penetrate to the very depths of my heart and soul. So be it.

AFFIRMATION # 21

With the infinite power and help of God, Jesus Christ, the Holy Ghost, and with intense faith, gratitude, and unconditional love for them and they for me, I now choose to purge the unrighteous element of greed from my life forever. I will act on this very essential affirmation from this moment on and for eternity. This affirmation will penetrate to the very depths of my heart and soul. So be it.

AFFIRMATION # 22

With the infinite power and help of God, Jesus Christ, the Holy Ghost, and with intense faith, gratitude, and unconditional love for them and they for me, I now choose to purge the unrighteous element of hostility from my life forever. I will now act on this essential affirmation from this moment on and for eternity. This affirmation will penetrate to the very depths of my heart and soul. So be it

AFFIRMATION # 23

With the infinite power and help of God, Jesus Christ, the Holy Ghost, and with intense faith, gratitude, and unconditional love for them and they for me, I now choose to expunge and purge the unrighteous element of hate from my life forever. I will now act on this essential affirmation from this moment on and for eternity. This affirmation will penetrate to the very depths of my heart and soul. So be it.

AFFIRMATION # 24

With the infinite power and help of God, Jesus Christ, the Holy Ghost, and with intense faith, gratitude, and unconditional love for them and they for me, I now choose to purge the unrighteous element of intolerance from my life forever. I will now act on this very essential affirmation from this moment on and for eternity. This affirmation will penetrate to the very depths of my heart and soul. So be it.

AFFIRMATION # 25

With the infinite power and help of God, Jesus Christ, the Holy Ghost, and with intense faith, gratitude, and unconditional love for them and they for me, I now choose to purge the unrighteous element of irreverence from my life forever, I will now act on this very essential affirmation from this moment on and forever. This affirmation will penetrate to the very depths of my heart and soul. So be it.

AFFFIRMATION # 26

With the infinite power and help of God, Jesus Christ, the Holy Ghost, and with intense faith, gratitude, and unconditional love for them and they for me, I now choose to purge the unrighteous element of insincerity from my life forever. I will now act on this essential affirmation from this moment on and for eternity. This affirmation will penetrate to the very depths of my heart and soul. So be it.

AFFIRMATION # 27

With the infinite power and help of God, Jesus Christ, the Holy Ghost, and with intense faith, gratitude and unconditional love for them and they for me, I now choose to purge the unrighteous element of jealousy from my life forever. I will now act on this very essential affirmation from this moment on and for eternity. This affirmation will penetrate to the very depths of my heart and soul. So be it.

AFFIRMATION # 28

With the infinite power and help of God, Jesus Christ, the Holy Ghost, and with intense faith, gratitude, and unconditional love for them and they for me, I now choose to purge the unrighteous element of laziness from my life forever. I will now act on this essential affirmation from this moment on and for eternity. This affirmation will penetrate to the very depths of my heart and soul. So be it.

AFFIRMATION # 29

With the infinite power and help of God, Jesus Christ, the Holy Ghost, and with intense faith, gratitude, and unconditional love for them and they for me I now choose to purge the unrighteous element of lying from my life forever. I will now act on this very essential affirmation from this moment on and for eternity. This affirmation will penetrate to the very depths of my heart and soul. So be it.

AFFIRMATION # 30

With the infinite power and help of God, Jesus Christ, the Holy Ghost, and with intense faith, gratitude, and unconditional love for them and they for me, I now choose to purge the unrighteous element of lust from my life forever. I will now act on this very essential affirmation from now on and for eternity. This affirmation will penetrate to the very depths of my heart and soul. So be it.

AFFIRMATION # 31

With the infinite power and help of God, Jesus Christ, the Holy Ghost, and with intense faith, gratitude, and unconditional love for them and they for me, I now choose to purge the unrighteous element of malevolence from my life forever. I will now act on this very essential affirmation from now on and for eternity. This affirmation will penetrate to the very depths of my heart and soul. So be it.

AFFIRMATION # 32

With the infinite power and help of God, Jesus Christ, the Holy Ghost, and with intense faith, gratitude, and unconditional love for them and they for me I now choose to purge the unrighteous element of malice from my life forever. I will now act on this very essential affirmation from now on and for eternity. This affirmation will penetrate to the very depths of my heart and soul. So be it.

AFFIRMATION # 33

With the infinite power and help of God, Jesus Christ, the Holy Ghost, and with intense faith, gratitude and unconditional love for them and they for me, I now choose to purge the unrighteous element of meanness from my life forever. I will now act on this very essential affirmation from now on and for eternity. This affirmation will penetrate to the very depths of my heart and soul. So be it.

AFFIRMATION # 34

With the infinite power and help of God, Jesus Christ, the Holy Ghost, and with intense faith, gratitude, and unconditional love for them and they for me, I now choose to purge the unrighteous element of negativity from my life forever. I will now act on this very essential affirmation form now on and for eternity. This affirmation will penetrate to the very depths of my heart and soul. So be it.

AFFIRMATION # 35

With the infinite power and help of God, Jesus Christ, the Holy Ghost, and with intense faith, gratitude, and unconditional love for them and they for me, I now choose to purge the unrighteous element of uncaring from my life forever. I will now act on this very essential affirmation from now on and for eternity. This affirmation will penetrate to the very depths of my heart and soul. So be it.

AFFIRMATION # 36

With the infinite power and help of God, Jesus Christ, the Holy Ghost, and with intense faith, gratitude, and unconditional love for them and they for me, I now choose to purge the unrighteous element of Pollution from my life forever. I will now act on this very essential affirmation from now on and for eternity. This affirmation will penetrate to the very depths of my heart and soul. So be it.

AFFIRMATION # 37

With the infinite power and help of God, Jesus Christ, The Holy Ghost, and with intense faith, gratitude, and unconditional love for them and they for me, I now choose to purge the unrighteous element of prejudice from my life forever. I will now act on this very essential affirmation from now on and for eternity. This affirmation will penetrate to the very depths of my heart and soul. So be it.

AFFIRMATION # 38

With the infinite power and help of God, Jesus Christ, the Holy Ghost, and with intense faith, gratitude, and unconditional love for them and they for me, I now choose to purge the unrighteous element of pride from my life forever. I will now act on this very essential affirmation from now on and for eternity. This affirmation will penetrate to the very depths of my heart and soul. So be it.

AFFIRMATION # 39

With the infinite power and help of God, Jesus Christ, the Holy Ghost, and with intense faith, gratitude, and unconditional love for them and they for me, I now choose to purge the unrighteous element of procrastination from my life forever. I will now act on this very essential affirmation from now on and for eternity. This affirmation will penetrate to the very depths of my heart and soul. So be it.

AFFIRMATION # 40

With the infinite power and help of God, Jesus Christ, the Holy Ghost, and with intense faith, gratitude, and unconditional love for them and they for me, I now choose to purge the unrighteous element of retribution from my life forever. I will now act on this very essential affirmation from now on and for eternity. This affirmation will penetrate to the very depths of my heart and soul. So be it.

AFFIRMATION # 41

With the infinite power and help of God, Jesus Christ the Holy Ghost, and with intense faith, gratitude, and unconditional love for them and they for me, I now choose to purge the unrighteous element of sloppiness, from my life forever. I will now act on this very essential affirmation from now on and for eternity. This affirmation will penetrate to the very depths of my heart and soul. So be it.

AFFIRMATION # 42

With the infinite power and help of God, Jesus Christ, the Holy Ghost, and with intense faith, gratitude, and unconditional love for them and they for me, I now choose to purge the unrighteous element of selfishness from my life forever. I will now act on this very essential affirmation from now on and for eternity. This affirmation will penetrate to the very depths of my heart and soul. So be it.

AFFIRMATION # 43

With the infinite power and help of God, Jesus Christ, the Holy Ghost, and with intense faith, gratitude, and unconditional love for them and they for me, I now choose to purge the unrighteous element of slothfulness from my life forever. I will now act on this very essential affirmation from now on and for eternity. This affirmation will penetrate to the very depths of my heart and soul. So be it.

AFFIRMATION # 44

With the infinite power and help of God, Jesus Christ, the Holy Ghost, and with intense faith, gratitude, and unconditional love for them and they for me, I now choose to purge the unrighteous element of strife from my life forever. I will now act on this very essential affirmation from now on and for eternity. This affirmation will penetrate to the very depths of my heart and soul. So be it.

AFFIRMATION # 45

With the infinite power and help of God, Jesus Christ, the Holy Ghost, and with intense faith, gratitude, and unconditional love for them and they for me, I now choose to purge the unrighteous trait of surrendering to evil from my life forever. I will now act on this very essential affirmation from now on and for eternity. This affirmation will penetrate to the very depths of my heart and soul. So be it.

AFFIRMATION # 46

With the infinite power and help of God, Jesus Christ, the Holy Ghost, and with intense faith, gratitude, and unconditional love for them and they for me, I now choose to purge the unrighteous element of being tactless from my life forever. I will now act on this very essential affirmation from now on until eternity. This affirmation will penetrate to the very depths of my heart and soul. So be it.

AFFIRMATION # 47

With the infinite power and help of God, Jesus Christ, the Holy Ghost, and with intense faith, gratitude, and unconditional love for them and they for me, I now choose to purge the unrighteous element of being thoughtless from my life forever. I will now act on this very essential affirmation from now on until eternity. This affirmation will penetrate to the very depths of my heart and soul. So be it.

AFFIRMATION # 48

With the infinite power and help of God, Jesus Christ, the Holy Ghost, and with intense faith, gratitude, and unconditional love for them and they for me, I now choose to purge the unrighteous element of being thankless from my life forever. I will now act on this very essential affirmation from now on until eternity. This affirmation will penetrate to the very depths of my heart and soul. So be it.

AFFIRMATION # 49

With the infinite power and help of God, Jesus Christ, the Holy Ghost, and with intense faith, gratitude, and unconditional love for them and they for me, I now choose to purge the unrighteous trait of being thoughtless from my life forever. I will now act on this very essential affirmation from now on until eternity. This affirmation will penetrate to the very depths of my heart and soul. So be it.

AFFIRMATION # 50

With the infinite power and help of God, Jesus Christ, the Holy Ghost, and with intense faith, gratitude, and unconditional love for them and they for me, I now choose to purge the unrighteous element of ugliness from my life forever. I will now act on this very essential affirmation from now on until eternity. This affirmation will penetrate to the very depths of my heart and soul. So be it.

AFFIRMATION # 51

With the infinite power and help of God, Jesus Christ, the Holy Ghost, and with intense faith, gratitude, and unconditional love for them and they for me, I now choose to purge the unrighteous trait of being unchaste from my life forever. I will now act on this very essential affirmation from now on until eternity. This affirmation will penetrate to the very depths of my heart and soul. So be it.

AFFIRMATION # 52

With the infinite power and help of God, Jesus Christ, the Holy Ghost, and with intense faith, gratitude, and unconditional love for them and they for me, I now choose to purge the unrighteous trait of being undisciplined from my life forever. I will now act on this very essential affirmation from now until eternity. This affirmation will penetrate to the very depths of my heart and soul. So be it.

AFFIRMATION # 53

With the infinite power and help of God, Jesus Christ, the Holy Ghost, and with intense faith, gratitude, and unconditional love for them and they for me, I now choose to purge the unrighteous trait of not enduring to the end from my life forever. I will now act on this very essential affirmation from now on until eternity. This affirmation will penetrate to the very depths of my heart and soul. So be it.

AFFIRMATION # 54

With the infinite power and help of God, Jesus Christ, the Holy Ghost, and with intense faith, gratitude, and unconditional love for them and they for me, I now choose to purge the unrighteous element of un-forgiveness from my life forever. I will now act on this very essential affirmation from now on until eternity. This affirmation will penetrate to the very depths of my heart and soul. So be it.

AFFIRMATION # 55

With the infinite power and help of God, Jesus Christ, the Holy Ghost, and with intense faith, gratitude, and unconditional love for them and they for me, I now choose to purge the unrighteous trait of being unlawful from my life forever. I will now act on this very essential affirmation from now on until eternity. This affirmation will penetrate to the very depths of my heart and soul. So be it.

AFFIRMATION # 56

With the infinite power and help of God, Jesus Christ, the Holy Ghost, and with intense faith, gratitude, and unconditional love for them and they for me, I now choose to purge the unrighteous trait of being non-prayerful from my life forever. I will now act on this very essential affirmation from now on until eternity. This affirmation will penetrate to the very depths of my heart and soul. So be it.

AFFIRMATION # 57

With the infinite power and help of God, Jesus Christ, the Holy Ghost, and with intense faith, gratitude, and unconditional love for them and they for me, I now choose to purge the unrighteous trait of being unprepared from my life forever. I will now act on this very essential affirmation from now on until eternity. This affirmation will penetrate to the very depths of my heart and soul. So be it.

AFFIRMATION # 58

With the infinite power and help of God, Jesus Christ, The Holy Ghost, and with intense faith, gratitude, and unconditional love for them and they for me, I now choose to purge the unrighteous trait of not seeking after knowledge from my life forever. I will now definitely seek for knowledge every day from now on until eternity. This affirmation will penetrate to the very depths of my heart and soul. So be it.

AFFIRMATION # 59

With the infinite power and help of God, Jesus Christ, the Holy Ghost, and with intense faith, gratitude, and unconditional love for them and they for me, I now choose to purge the unrighteous trait of being unrighteous from my life forever. I will now act on this very essential affirmation from now on until eternity. This affirmation will penetrate to the very depths of my heart and soul. So be it.

AFFIRMATION # 60

With the infinite power and help of God, Jesus Christ the Holy Ghost, and with intense faith, gratitude, and unconditional love for them and they for me, I now choose to purge the unrighteous trait of being unsuccessful from my life forever. I will now act on this very essential affirmation from now on until eternity. This affirmation will penetrate to the very depths of my heart and soul. So be it.

AFFIRMATION # 61

With the infinite power and help of God, Jesus Christ, the Holy Ghost, and with intense faith, gratitude, and unconditional love for them and they for me, I now choose to purge the unrighteous trait of not being teachable from my life forever. I will now act on this very essential affirmation from now on until eternity. This affirmation will penetrate to the very depths of my heart and soul. So be it.

AFFIRMATION # 62

With the infinite power and help of God, Jesus Christ, the Holy Ghost, and with intense faith, gratitude, and unconditional love for them and they for me, I now choose to purge the unrighteous trait of not being trustworthy from my life forever. I will now act on this very essential affirmation from now on until eternity. This affirmation will penetrate to the very depths of my heart and soul. So be it.

AFFIRMATION # 63

With the infinite power and help of God, Jesus Christ, the Holy Ghost, and with intense faith, gratitude, and unconditional love for them and they for me, I now choose to purge the unrighteous trait of not being virtuous from my life forever. I will now act on this very essential affirmation from now on until eternity. This affirmation will penetrate to the very depths of my heart and soul. So be it.

Chapter Twelve

EVEN MORE AFFIRMATION FORMATS

THE FOLLOWING AFFIRMATIONS ARE A FEW THAT I, PERSONALLY, HAVE USED VERY SUCCESSFULLY. I LEAVE YOU THESE, AND ALL OTHER AFFIRMATIONS, AND ASSERTIONS, IN THE HOPES THAT THEY WILL MAKE A VERY POSITIVE CHANGE, AND IMPACT ON YOUR LIFE. MAY GOD BE WITH YOU, AND BLESS YOU IN YOUR QUEST TO LIVE WITH HIM IN THE ETERNITIES.

AFFIRMATION # 1

WITH THE INFINITE, AND POWERFUL HELP OF GOD, JESUS CHRIST, THE HOLY GHOST, AND WITH UNWAVERING FAITH, GRATITUDE, AND UNCONDITIONAL LOVE FOR THEM AND THEY FOR ME, I NOW CHOOSE TO ACCEPT THEIR ETERNAL LOVE FOR ME, WITHOUT RESERVATION, WITH UNDYING THANKSGIVING AND UPON MY TOTAL ACCEPTANCE OF THEIR LOVE, I PLEDGE TO MAGNIFY, EXPAND, AND EXTEND TO ALL, MY LOVE, TO ENLIGHTEN THEIR LIVES AND EXPAND THEIR MINDS. I AM NOW EXTREMELY DETERMINED TO HONOR AND OBEY THIS VERY ESSENTIAL AFFIRMATION, WHICH WILL PENETRATE TO THE VERY DEPTHS OF MY SOUL AND SPIRIT, FROM THIS MOMENT ON AND FOREVER.

AFFIRMATION # 2

WITH THE INFINITE, AND POWERFUL HELP OF GOD, JESUS CHRIST, THE HOLY GHOST, AND WITH UNWAVERING FAITH, GRATITUDE, AND UNCONDITIONAL LOVE FOR THEM, AND THEY FOR ME, AND WITH THEIR HELP AND APPROVAL I NOW CHOOSE TO EXPAND ALL OF MY ABILITIES AND CALL ON THE GREAT HEALING POWER OF DEITY, TO HEAL MY KNEES, HIPS AND ALL OTHER MALADIES AND RID ME OF MY PAIN AND HEADACHES. THIS GREAT HEALING POWER WILL REBUILD THE NORMAL CARTILAGE IN MY DEFECTIVE JOINTS. I AM NOW EXTREMELY DETERMINED TO HONOR AND OBEY THIS VERY ESSENTIAL AFFIRMATION, WHICH WILL PENETRATE TO THE VERY DEPTHS OF MY SOUL AND SPIRIT, FROM THIS MOMENT ON AND FOREVER. SO BE IT.

AFFIRMATION # 3

WITH THE INFINITELY, POWERFUL HELP OF GOD, JESUS CHRIST, THE HOLY GHOST, AND WITH HUMILITY, UNWAVERING FAITH, GRATITUDE, AND UNCONDITIONAL LOVE FOR THEM AND THEY FOR ME, AND WITH THEIR HELP AND APPROVAL I NOW CHOOSE TO DEVELOP A PROFOUND FEELING OF LOVE FOR DEITY, AND ALL MANKIND. WITH DEEP, PENETRATING THANKFULNESS I NOW ASK THEM FOR THE STRENGTH AND PERCEPTION REQUIRED TO RID MYSELF OF THE FEAR AND ANGER ASSOCIATED WITH PHYSICAL AND MENTAL EVENTS THAT OCCURED DURING MY CHILDHOOD. I AM NOW EXTREMELY DETERMINED TO HONOR AND OBEY THIS AFFIRMATION, WHICH WILL PENETRATE TO THE VERY DEPTHS OF MY SOUL AND SPIRIT, FROM THIS MOMENT ON AND FOREVER. SO BE IT.

AFFIRMATION # 4

WITH THE INFINITELY POWERFUL HELP OF GOD, JESUS CHRIST, THE HOLY GHOST, AND UNWAVERING FAITH, GRATITUDE, AND UNCONDITIONAL LOVE FOR THEM AND THEY FOR ME, AND WITH THEIR APPROVAL WE NOW CHOOSE TO RID ME OF ALL BELIEFS, WHICH AFFECT MY ABILITIES, FAITH, MY SPSIRITUAL GROWTH, AND ON ALL OF MY UNDEVELOPED TALENTS. I AM NOW EXTREMELY DETERMINED TO HONOR AND OBEY THIS VERY ESSENTIAL AFFIRMATION, WHICH WILL PENETRATE TO THE VERY DEPTHS OF MY SOUL AND SPIRIT, FROM THIS MOMENT ON AND FOREVER. SO BE IT.

AFFIRMATION # 5

WITH THE INFINITELY POWERFUL HELP OF GOD, JESUS CHRIST, THE HOLY GHOST, AND WITH UNWAVERING FAITH, GRATITUDE, HUMILITY AND UNCONDITIONAL LOVE FOR THEM AND THEY FOR ME, AND WITH THEIR APPROVAL WE NOW CHOOSE TO RID ME OF ANY CHARECTERISTIC OR TRAIT THAT AFFECTS MY SPIRITUAL GROWTH. I AM EXTREMELY DETERMINED TO HONOR AND OBEY THIS VERY ESSENTIAL AFFIRMATION, WHICH WILL PENETRATE TO THE VERY DEPTHS OF MY SOUL AND SPIRIT, FROM THIS MOMENT ON AND FOREVER. SO BE IT.

Chapter Thirteen

MY PERSONAL TESTIMONY

MAY WE ALL TREAT EACH day and each other as sacred, Holy gifts of Heavenly Father, by righteously, using our knowledge, wisdom, intelligence, and talents, to magnify and expand each of them to bring us closer to God. May we create this day and each other as very righteous monuments to God and be as productive and obedient as we can possibly be. Happiness comes from obedience.

I give my love to all who read, ponder and act on the information presented in these pages. Let us all identify, overcome, conquer, and rise above all afflictions, adversities, illnesses and problems, with the help of God, Jesus Christ and the Holy. Ghost, and may your efforts bring you back into Deities s presence. All three of them bless each of us in our every day righteous endeavors.

Chapter Fourteen

GOD REALLY DOES EXIST!

I HAVE OFTEN BEEN ASKED why God allows so much pain, sorrow, and suffering of mankind. The following partially answers this question. Since man is so limited in his thinking, compared to God, in this life we may never know all the answers. God looks on death much differently than do we mortals. Only He knows the reasons for the pain and suffering some of us go through. I will never second-guess these reasons, because I lack the knowledge, wisdom and intelligence to have the required answers.

Man's pain and suffering, because of wars, illness, accidents, terrible childhood events, etc. is difficult for we mortals to comprehend or explain. The following is my partial explanation. God has given man his agency, (the right to make choices as he sees fit), I believe that God allows, or initiates these adversities for the following reasons:

Most importantly, to remind us of the terrible suffering Jesus Christ endured, for the salvation and exaltation of His children. Our suffering can never equal the pain He endured. We, sometimes, get a touch of His great pain, and consequently, we are able to have partial empathy with Him.

The reasons, it is to:

1. Show us what happens when we don't rely on Him for protection.
2. Humble us.
3. Help us know that Deity does exist.
4. Encourage us to repent.
5. Encourage us to develop faith in Deity

DR. LAUREN J. BALL

6. Encourage our obedience to Gods laws and commandments.
7. Encourage us to search for the truth and only base our beliefs on proven truths, found mostly, in the scriptures.
8. Encourage us to rely on and gain His protection and show His love for each of us.
9. It is to let us know, that through obedience and faith, Deity can bring relief from pain and suffering.
10. Encourage and help us to accomplish His goals for His children.

For those who knew the light and now believe there is no God, are gambling their eternal lives, that God doesn't exist; in spite of all the evidence that He does?

If God doesn't exist it will make no difference in our beliefs. If we die, this life is all there is. There is no hope, and no future, so why are we here in the first place?

But if God does exist, **and He does**, then there is hope and faith that we, His children, may have, through obedience, repentance, and spiritual growth, all that He has;

His knowledge, wisdom, intelligence, power, and glory and enjoy eternal life with Him. If God, Christ, and the Holy Ghost have been denied, after having known them, then at the final judgment, the deniers and disbelievers, and those who have rebelled, may all be cast into outer darkness with Lucifer, and his hoards.

Should we, then, really, gamble with our lives and others lives, who may decide to follow our lead? Do we really want to reside with Lucifer forever?

God's knowledge, intelligence, wisdom, power, and glory are so far above ours that we puny humans cannot begin to comprehend all of the reasons why God allows, and does, what he does. The scriptures explain many reasons why they exist, why He does, what He does. Even with the scriptures, we know only a small part of His eternal plans for us.

All of the miracles I have experienced in my lifetime, through wars and recovering from many adversities, afflictions, and feeling the hand, and love, of God in every aspect of my life, proves to me, beyond a shadow of a doubt, that God does exist, that He loves as no man can love, and He only wants what is best for us.

Last of all I bare you my testimony that God, Jesus Christ and the Holy Ghost really do exist, and through their great love they are here to guide and direct our lives, if we learn to listen. Their love shines down from their residence, and bathes each of us equally and continually. The difference in each of us is the quality and quantity we accept from Them, and extend to all others.

I have a hope and the faith that will encourage, and sustain me to be a better person, and to love everyone. The love I receive from above and the hope and faith I have received from Deity, will sustain me through all the adversities we go through here on earth. This hope, faith and love helps me grow spiritually and brings satisfaction and joy to my soul and encourages me to remain in a state of repentance daily.

Without love, faith, hope and charity I would have no promise. My life would have no meaning. There would be no reason to exist except to live from day to day, and maybe strive for riches, knowing that my efforts would bear no spiritual fruit. All I would have in the end, after death, would be a great nothingness in the eternities. What an existence to look forward to.

Our knowledge of God comes through every scripture ever written, through men and women who have actually seen Him and have born witness that He does, indeed, really exist.

What credible witness can the unbeliever produce that God does not exist? What future can they possibly hope for? What a meaningless existence to have to live through!

Besides the many witnesses that have been given, without any recompense, I submit that every living thing on earth, every rock, waterfall, the oceans, in fact every inanimate and animate object on this earth and in the heavens, are testimonies of His existence and His love for us. Yes, God does live. **I have seen Him personally, in all His glory**. I testify that this is true in the sacred name of Jesus Christ. Amen.

It is my prayer that those who desire to improve their spiritual lives, will use the therapies, assertions and affirmation in this book to help them, in righteousness; *identify, overcome, conquer, and rise above all their adversities, afflictions, imperfections, and maladies, all, with the help of God, Jesus Christ, and the Holy Ghost.*

May God bless all of your righteous efforts! So be it.

Printed in the United States
By Bookmasters